BUTTERFLIES

text by
RONALD ORENSTEIN

photography by
THOMAS MARENT

FIREFLY BOOKS

A FIREFLY BOOK

Published by Firefly Books Ltd. © 2015
Text Copyright © 2015 Ronald Orenstein
Photography Copyright © 2015 Thomas Marent
(except as listed at right)

First printing

Publisher Cataloging-in-Publication Data (U.S.)

Orenstein, Ronald I. (Ronald Isaac), 1946–
   Butterflies / text by Ronald Orenstein ; photography by Thomas Marent.
[288] pages : color photographs ; cm.
Includes bibliographical references and index.
Summary: Stunning photography provides a close-up look at the remarkable Order Lepidoptera. The macro photography is complemented by text which explains the latest scientific discoveries about these wonderful insects.
ISBN-13: 978-1-77085-580-9
1. Butterflies – Pictorial works. I. Marent, Thomas. II. Title.
595.78 dc23   QL543.O635   2015

Library and Archives Canada Cataloguing in Publication

Marent, Thomas, photographer
   Butterflies / Thomas Marent, photographer ; Ronald Orenstein, author of text.
 Includes bibliographical references and index.
ISBN 978-1-77085-580-9 (bound)
   1. Butterflies – Pictorial works. 2. Butterflies.
I. Orenstein, Ronald I. (Ronald Isaac), 1946– , author
II. Title.
 QL542.M37 2015   595.78'9   C2015-903440-X

Photo captions, preliminary pages:
Title page spread: European Peacock (*Aglais* [*Inachis*] *io*), Switzerland (Nymphalidae: Nymphalinae)

Contents spread: Purple Sapphire (*Heliophorus epicles*), India (Lycaenidae: Lycaeninae)

Published in the United States by
Firefly Books (U.S.) Inc.
P.O. Box 1338, Ellicott Station
Buffalo, New York 14205

Published in Canada by
Firefly Books Ltd.
50 Staples Avenue, Unit 1
Richmond Hill, Ontario L4B 0A7

Cover and interior design: Counterpunch Inc./Linda Gustafson

Printed in China

The publisher gratefully acknowledges the financial support for our publishing program by the Government of Canada through the Canada Book Fund as administered by the Department of Canadian Heritage.

Photo Credits

All photos copyright © 2015 Thomas Marent except for the following:

Dreamstime
Page 14 © John Anderson / Dreamstime.com
Page 17 © Jason P. Ross / Dreamstime.com
Page 18 © Stevenrussellsmithphotos / Dreamstime.com

National Geographic Creative
Pages 8–9 © DARLYNE A. MURAWSKI / National Geographic Creative
Page 25 © AMY WHIT & AL PETTEWAY / National Geographic Creative
Pages 31, 34a, b, c, d, 35 © JOEL SARTORE / National Geographic Creative

Nature Picture Library
Page 15 © Steven David Miller / naturepl.com
Page 16 © Kim Taylor / naturepl.com
Page 21 © Rolf Nussbaumer / naturepl.com
Page 22 © Michael Durham / naturepl.com
Page 29 © Thomas Lazar / naturepl.com
Page 33 © Shattil & Rozinski / naturepl.com

Ronald Orenstein
Pages 13, 26, 27, 28 © Ronald Orenstein

Other
Page 11 © Museum of Comparative Zoology, Harvard University
Page 12 (both) © Dr. Luc Legal
Page 24 © Ryan Kaldari / Wikimedia Commons

For Royce

Ronald Orenstein

For my parents

Thomas Marent

Contents

Introducing Butterflies

It would be nice to think that butterflies had something to do with butter, like the bread-and-butterfly Alice encounters behind the looking-glass. The Old English word *buttorfleoge*, from which "butterfly" probably derives, may have been inspired by the butter-yellow wings of the Brimstone (*Gonepteryx rhamni*). It may also come from the belief that butterflies hovering around milk pails were actually witches in disguise, there to steal the cream. The peculiar word "caterpillar" is supposed to come from the Old French *chatepelose*, meaning "hairy cat" or, roughly, "fuzzball." Or maybe it comes from *cate*, meaning "food," and *piller*, meaning "pillage," in recognition of its voracious appetite. We don't know for sure.

Papilio glaucus *and* Battus philenor, Great Smoky Mountains National Park, Tennessee, USA (Papilionidae: Papilioninae)
A cluster of Eastern Tiger Swallowtails (*Papilio glaucus*) puddles for minerals in a patch of damp soil, joined by a single male Pipevine Swallowtail (*Battus philenor*). Some female Eastern Tiger Swallowtails, but not males, are mimics of the distasteful Pipevine Swallowtail.

Butterflies have long been symbols of our own ephemeral nature. To the Blackfoot, butterflies are the bringers of dreams. According to the creation myths of the Miao people of southwestern China, the human race itself is descended from the eggs of a Butterfly Mother. In China butterflies are symbols of long life, beauty and elegance. A pair of butterflies symbolizes eternal love, most famously in the 1,600-year-old legend of the "butterfly lovers" Liang Shanbo and Zhu Yingtai, who were turned into butterflies after their tragic deaths.

Butterfly life cycles are metaphors for birth, death and rebirth for peoples from Japan to Mexico. The arrival of Monarch butterflies (*Danaus plexippus*) on their wintering grounds in Mexico coincides with the Day of the Dead (*Día de los Muertos*), and Mexicans have traditionally viewed the arriving insects as the souls of their ancestors, come for their yearly visit. The pre-Columbian flower goddess Xochiquetzal, worshipped as an aspect of a lunar cult in central Mexico, was identified with the Two-tailed Swallowtail (*Papilio multicaudatus*) because of both its attraction to flowers and its aggressive, warrior-like nature, since Xochiquetzal was a warrior herself.

Butterflies have become model organisms for studies in genetics, ecology and evolutionary biology. Engineers have tried to replicate their flight. Designers of antifogging and antifouling surfaces, which are needed for everything from medical catheters to nuclear power plants, have analyzed the way a butterfly's wings direct water droplets away from its body. The intricately structured, dazzlingly iridescent wing scales of tropical American morphos (*Morpho* spp.) have been examined, particularly in China, for their application to the design of reflective surfaces and – because exposure to different gases changes their iridescent tint – vapor detectors.

For centuries, then, we have seen butterflies as remarkable creatures. And we are still learning how remarkable they are.

What Are Butterflies?

Butterflies are insects. They have the standard combination of features that define insects as animals: an outer covering, or exoskeleton, made from a polysaccharide called chitin; a body divided into head, thorax and abdomen; six jointed legs attached to the thorax; a breathing system based on a series of tubes, or tracheae, that run through the body and open along the side through a series of breathing holes, or spiracles; a pair of antennae on the head; and an open circulatory system supplied by a heart that pumps a fluid called hemolymph through the animal's body. As in most insect lineages, adult butterflies have multifaceted compound eyes and two pairs of wings, the forewings and hindwings, which arise from the second and third segments of the thorax.

Butterflies are moths. That statement may surprise you, but in an evolutionary sense butterflies are a single day–flying branch – one that contains some 17,500 species in 6, or perhaps 7 families – of a moth family tree with roughly 200,000 members in more than 125 families. Butterflies and moths belong to the order Lepidoptera, or "scaly wings," named for the tiny overlapping scales that cover their wings. Butterflies are part of an advanced moth lineage that contains 99% of living lepidopteran species. Except for a very few ancient moth families, adult lepidopterans lack functional chewing mandibles. Most have instead a coiled "tongue," or proboscis, adapted to feeding on nectar and other liquids. The easiest way to tell butterflies from other moths is to look at the antennae. Most moth antennae are either plain-tipped or feather-like, while almost (but not quite) all butterfly antennae are tipped with club-like knobs, surmounted in the skippers (Hesperiidae) with whisker-like extensions.

Butterflies and moths are holometabolous, meaning that they go through four life stages: egg, larva, pupa and adult. Holometabolous insects, collectively known as Endopterygota, include flies (Diptera), beetles (Coleoptera) and bees, wasps and ants (Hymenoptera), as well as a number of smaller orders, including the one closest to butterflies and moths, the caddisflies (Trichoptera). There are some 850,000 of them – more than half of all the known species of animals on Earth.

The Rise of Butterflies

There have been butterflies for as long as there have been flowers. Their rise accompanied a great evolutionary event: the diversification and spread of angiosperms, the flowering plants that dominate Earth today. Flowers enticed insects to carry their pollen, and they rewarded them with nectar. Millions of years later they would be visited by nectar-feeding birds and bats, but the opportunity to partner with flowers was first taken up by the insects.

The most primitive moths today have functional chewing jaws even as adults, and caterpillars that feed on nonflowering plants such as mosses and conifers. The switch to angiosperms and their flowers took place after moths first appeared. The fossil record of butterflies and moths is sparse and tells us little about their history, but recent studies using molecular "clocks" to measure the timing of evolutionary change suggest that the Lepidoptera and their nearest relatives, the caddisflies, branched off from one another in the late Triassic period, about 230 million years ago. *Archaeolepis mane*, the earliest known

Prodryas persephone, Florissant Fossil Beds, Colorado, USA (Nymphalidae: Nymphalinae)
This 34- to 37-million-year-old fossil, collected in Colorado in the 1870s by homesteader Charlotte Hill, is the only known specimen of the Persephone Nymphalid (*Prodryas persephone*). It is one of the best-preserved fossil butterflies in existence; even the scales on its forewing can be distinguished.

Baronia b. brevicornis female, Cerro Frio, Morelos, Mexico (left) and male, Quilamula, Morelos, Mexico (right) (Papilionidae: Baroniinae)

The Archaic Swallowtail or Short-horned Baronia (*Baronia brevicornis*) of central Mexico is the sole survivor of an ancient butterfly lineage. It is the only swallowtail whose caterpillars feed regularly on *Acacia* leaves like these.

fossil moth, dates from the early Jurassic, 190 million years ago. Modern butterflies probably first appeared in the early Cretaceous period, when flowering plants were undergoing their major evolutionary spurt. Butterflies and flowering plants were both well established by the late Cretaceous, the time of the oldest known butterfly fossil. By then adult butterflies were almost certainly drinking from angiosperm flowers and their caterpillars were eating angiosperm leaves.

Traces of butterfly evolutionary history can be seen in the plants their larvae eat. Butterflies tend to be very conservative about the host plants their caterpillars feed on. Once they have adapted to the particular chemistry of one plant family, they are likely to stay with it for some time. However, butterfly lineages have switched from one plant group to another and, sometimes, back again. Skipper larvae, for instance, feed mostly upon monocots: grasses and palms, for example. The shift to these plants may have occurred only once, but today more than half of all skipper caterpillars feed on grasses and their relatives.

Nonetheless, their usual conservatism allows us to make some guesses about the ancestral butterfly and its original host plant. We now believe that swallowtails (Papilionidae) represent the oldest living butterfly lineage. Based on what some swallowtail caterpillars eat today, it has been suggested that their ancestral host plants may have been related to Dutchman's pipe (Family Aristolochiaceae). The caterpillars of the most "primitive" of living swallowtails, the Archaic Swallowtail or Short-horned Baronia (*Baronia brevicornis*) of Mexico, eat *Acacia* leaves, but acacias probably did not exist when *Baronia* arose some 68 million years ago. Its nearest relatives lay eggs on members of the stonecrop family (Crassulaceae), a plant group as old as *Baronia* itself, so the first butterfly caterpillars may have dined on ancient stonecrops.

Butterfly Families

Butterflies were once divided into many families, but today scientists recognize no more than six: swallowtails (Papilionidae), skippers (Hesperiidae), whites and yellows (Pieridae), brush-footed butterflies (Nymphalidae), gossamer-winged butterflies (Lycaenidae) and metalmarks (Riodinidae, previously classified as a subfamily of the Lycaenidae). There is still some question as to how closely the skippers are related to other butterflies. The classical approach has been to include all the other butterfly families in a superfamily, the Papilionoidea, with the skippers as their closest cousins but in a separate superfamily, the Hesperioidea. If, as recent molecular studies suggest, the swallowtails rather than the skippers were the first family to split from the main butterfly line, then the skippers belong within the Papilionoidea.

The situation was complicated in the 1980s by the realization (later confirmed by molecular studies) that a small family of tropical American insects, the butterfly moths (Hedylidae), may not be moths that just happen to be butterfly-like but a very early lineage of butterflies that either took up or retained a nocturnal lifestyle (though at least two species also fly by day). Hedylid adults look like typical – if slimly built and long-winged – moths with either hair-like or feather-like (not clubbed) antennae. Their caterpillars and pupae, however, have a number of butterfly-like features, including a swallowtail-like silken girdle used to suspend the chrysalis. There are only about 35 to 40 known species of hedylids, all in the genus *Macrosoma*. They are now usually placed in their own superfamily, the Hedyloidea, as the closest living relatives of the Papilionoidea. One recent study suggests that hedylids actually belong within the Papilionoidea, as the closest relatives of the skippers. If that theory proves correct, it will mean that their moth-like features (and nocturnal behavior) were acquired secondarily as they evolved from a day-flying butterfly ancestor.

The swallowtails may have arisen some 110 million years ago, followed five million years later by the whites. The huge family Nymphalidae, the brush-footed butterflies, probably appeared three million years after that. The modern families would all have been established by the time the gossamer-wings split from the metalmarks

some 88 million years ago. By the end of the Cretaceous, 65 million years ago, the Nymphalidae had already split into subfamilies. A time-traveling visitor to the last days of the dinosaurs would have encountered all the butterfly families we see today.

***Macrosoma nigrimacula*, Manu National Park, Peru (Hedylidae)**
Butterfly moths (Family Hedylidae) such as this *Macrosoma nigrimacula* are either butterflies' closest relatives, or true butterflies that took up a mostly nocturnal, moth-like lifestyle.

Wings and Flight

A butterfly's wing is a double-layered membrane supported by a radiating network of hollow tubular veins. Nerves and respiratory tubes, or tracheae, run through the veins, and a newly emerged butterfly pumps hemolymph through them as its wings expand. Membranous sheets, or cells, stretch between the veins; experts use names and numbers to describe the arrangement of veins and cells on each wing. In many moths a connecting mechanism on the hindwing, the frenulum, attaches to a retinaculum on the forewing. Except for the Regent Skipper (*Euschemon rafflesia*) of Australia, no butterfly possesses a frenulum or a retinaculum. In other butterflies (and larger moths) the wings overlap enough to function as a single unit without a connecting mechanism, particularly in gliding flight.

Vanessa virginiensis, USA (Nymphalidae: Nymphalinae)

The American Lady (*Vanessa virginiensis*) winters in the southern United States and migrates northward into Canada each spring. Like its cousin the Painted Lady (*V. cardui*), it is a strong flyer.

wall, levering the wings around a fulcrum. One pair pulls the thorax from front to back, buckling its upper surface upward; this movement drives the wing downward. The other draws the top and bottom of the thorax together, buckling the thoracic wall in the opposite direction and driving the wings upward again. The second set of muscles sets the whole system vibrating, leaving the first with much less to do. This indirect flight mechanism apparently evolved as insects acquired the ability to fold their wings – allowing a beetle, for example, to tuck its hindwings under the hard shell formed by its forewings. Dragonflies lack this ability, and butterflies have lost it.

Butterflies, with their four flat wings, do not fly like birds (though the flight of hummingbirds comes close). Their wings provide lift by creating vortices of air at their leading edges. Because butterfly wings are relatively large, the downstroke provides more lift than the butterfly needs, which is why butterflies tend to bob into the air at each stroke. Their flight is truly smooth and stable only on takeoff, when almost the whole body is involved in getting the insect into the air. Once aloft, they gain some stability, particularly in windy weather, because their wings bend with each beat, taking up energy that might otherwise cause them to tumble out of control. Erratic flight has benefits. It makes butterflies harder for a predator to catch, and for iridescent butterflies such as morphos, it may enhance the heliographic, on-and-off flashing effect that sunlight creates when it strikes their wings.

The flight of the Painted Lady (*Vanessa cardui*), a strong-flying long-distance migrant and the world's most widely distributed butterfly, has caught the attention of the United States Air Force. The USAF funds research into butterfly flight mechanics. It is less interested in natural history than in the prospect of developing tiny flying robots (micro aerial vehicles, or MAVs) that can imitate a butterfly's extreme maneuverability in the air.

Painted Ladies flap their wings about 20 to 25 times per second. The Large White (*Pieris brassicae*) flaps as slowly as 10 beats per second, too slow to support hovering flight – that's why butterflies generally don't hover. Some tiny wasps, by contrast, beat their wings at 400 times per second and hover quite well. In calm weather butterflies rarely flap their wings continuously. After a

Wings have unexpected functions. Male crackers (*Hamadryas* spp.) use two swollen forewing veins to make loud snapping noises in flight. Each contains an internal spiral structure that either buckles independently or strikes the other when the wings meet. The "ear" that hears them – Vogel's organ – is another structure on the wing.

Butterfly flight muscles are not attached to the wings themselves. In all but the oldest insect groups (such as dragonflies), the wings are attached to the thoracic wall through a lever mechanism that works like a tiny see-saw. Two pairs of muscles alter the shape of the thoracic eries of flaps, they will usually hold their wings upward in a V position and glide forward until they start to flap again. This makes their flight much more efficient than it would be if every forward motion required a powered wing-beat (a point not lost on the designers of MAVs).

Johns Hopkins University graduate student Tiras Lin used high-speed videography to analyze the Painted Lady's twists and turns in flight. In 2012 Lin discovered that the butterflies use their wings the way a spinning skater uses her arms. When a skater draws her arms close to her body, she spins faster, and when she extends them, she slows down. The arm movements redistribute her weight and alter her moment of inertia, a measure that determines how quickly she can spin. Butterflies seem able to do the same with their wings. So do birds, but butterfly wings were supposed to be too light to affect their overall weight distribution. Lin's studies proved that this assumption was not true, even though its wings account for only about 7% of a Painted Lady's body weight.

Scales and Colors

Butterfly wing membranes are covered on both sides with thousands of tiny overlapping scales; these are

Eumaeus atala, **Naples Botanical Gardens, Florida, USA (Lycaenidae: Theclinae)**
The Atala (*Eumaeus atala*), found in southern Florida, the Bahamas and Cuba, is one of North America's most colorful hairstreaks. Its pattern combines deep, melanin-rich blacks, red pigmented areas, and iridescent blue structural colors resulting when light is refracted by specialized wing scales.

in butterflies such as the Ulysses Swallowtail (*Papilio*

much the same way. The ridges on their iridescence-producing scales are packed together at up to 2,000 per millimeter. In most morphos these scales are part of the ground layer rather than the cover layer, and the cover layer is missing altogether in the Sickle-winged Morpho (*M. rhetenor*). Morpho wings are very large for their body size. When a morpho does land, it folds its wings tightly, leaving only its mottled brown underside visible, but in flight their iridescence is a challenge to rivals, catching the sunlight in repeated flashes as they fly; one way to attract a male morpho is to wave a blue silk scarf.

Wing Patterns and Genetics

Each scale on a butterfly's wing, like a pixel on a computer screen, displays a single color. The genetic instructions that set out its pattern are akin to computer code, setting the color of each scale to paint an "onscreen" two-dimensional image. Scientists in the relatively new field of evolutionary developmental biology ("evo-devo" for short) use butterfly wing patterns to study the ways in which blueprints in genes are translated into differentiated structures in our bodies.

In the 1920s two scientists, Boris Schwanwitsch

***Junonia coenia*, Distillery Conservation Area, Illinois, USA (Nymphalidae: Nymphalinae)**
The large, realistic eyespots on the wings of the Common Buckeye (*Junonia coenia*), a widespread North American butterfly, probably evolved from a row of smaller, circular dots. The more they resembled real eyes, the better they may have served to scare off hungry birds.

Thanks to laboratory research on a much-studied African butterfly, the Squinting Bush Brown (*Bicyclus anynana*), we now know that one gene – paradoxically called *wingless* (*wg*) – is central to wing-pattern formation. *Wingless* generates a protein – also called Wingless, but without the italics – that acts as a morphogen, a generator and controller of developmental change. The Wingless protein is produced near the margin of the wing and spreads inward toward the base and outward to the rim. As it spreads, each developing scale receives different concentrations of morphogen. The level of concentration that each receives signals the color it will eventually be. Wingless is not the only butterfly morphogen; others may be crucial in different butterfly species, but the process involved is basically the same.

What about the eyespots? Why do we suddenly get, not stripes running parallel to the wing margin, but circles surrounding a central focus? This has become a key evo-devo question. One suggestion is that a mutation broke up a band of tissue, reducing the Wingless morphogen to a series of isolated dots. Within this band the morphogen now spreads outward from each dot like ripples in a pond. The developing scales around it are "fooled" into assembling themselves into colored rings instead of a single band. This change from bands to eyespots may have happened very quickly. If an eyespot grows big enough to startle a predator, selection may act on it to increase its resemblance to a real vertebrate eye.

***Limenitis archippus*, USA (Nymphalidae: Limenitidinae)**
Over most of its range, the Viceroy (*Limenitis archippus*) is a mimic of the Monarch butterfly (*Danaus plexippus*). The most obvious difference is the black band across the middle of the hindwing in the Viceroy.

Mimics and Models

The Monarch butterfly (*Danaus plexippus*) is famously unpalatable. At least twice in their history (three times for the Monarchs themselves), Monarchs and their relatives underwent genetic changes that gave them an increased ability to tolerate toxic plant compounds called cardenolides. Their larvae could now dine on cardenolide-rich milkweeds and store the toxins in their own systems. Both larvae and adults became toxic meal choices for otherwise hungry birds. The butterflies evolved aposematic, or warning, colors, and birds learned to avoid them.

This handed other butterflies an evolutionary opportunity. If they could convince "educated" birds that they too were Monarchs, they might be safe. A bird that had tasted a Monarch and was unwilling to risk another unpleasant experience might avoid a palatable lookalike

Other unpalatable butterflies could shorten a predator's learning curve if they copied the Monarch's warning pattern instead of developing one of their own.

That, in a nutshell, has been the basis for one of the most widespread, repeated, remarkable and thoroughly studied phenomena of butterfly evolution: the extensive – and often amazingly accurate – mimicry of one butterfly species by another. Mimicry has been conveniently divided into two types, though the differences between them are rarely clear-cut. The great 19th-century naturalist, explorer and travel writer Henry Walter Bates was the first to describe Batesian mimicry, in which a toxic or distasteful model is imitated by a perfectly palatable mimic. In Müllerian mimicry, first described in 1879 by the German-Brazilian naturalist Fritz Müller, both species are toxic, face the same predator and copy each other.

North American admirals (*Limenitis* spp.) have evolved into mimics at least three times (and have lost their mimicry at least once). The Viceroy (*L. archippus*) mimics the Monarch, except in the southern United States, where a darker form mimics the Monarch's mahogany-colored cousins the Queen (*Danaus gilippus*) and the Soldier (*D. eresimus*). Long considered a Batesian mimic, it may be distasteful itself.

In the tropics there are whole complexes, or rings, of mimics so much like one another that even a trained observer – or an experienced predator – may have trouble telling them apart. In Central and South America there are mimicry rings involving some 200 species of amazingly similar long-winged orange, black and yellow "tiger mimics." They include butterflies from several families, moths and even a genus of damselfly. In Southeast Asia, swallowtails and day-flying moths imitate blackish, blue-striped Monarch relatives. Several mimicry rings may share the same Ecuadorian rainforest, flying at varying heights among the trees, each at the level where its larval food plants grow. Members of some South American mimicry rings roost together at night. Birds may be attracted to butterfly gatherings as they come together at dusk, and "educating" one predator that its butterflies are not worth eating may protect the others in the roost.

Batesian mimics must always be rarer that their models. If there are too many tasty mimics, a predator might never learn to avoid them. This may be why some Batesian mimics occur in a variety of forms, each copying a different model. That way, no one form can become too common. Müllerian mimics, which are toxic themselves, face no such constraints, though the Amazonian butterfly *Heliconius numata*, a mimic with up to seven coexisting forms, appears to be Müllerian.

In a number of swallowtails, and some whites, only the female is a mimic. The classic example is the Mocker Swallowtail (*Papilio dardanus*), whose females copy different butterflies in various parts of their African range. In North America most Eastern Tiger Swallowtails (*Papilio glaucus*) are contrastingly yellow and black, but a substantial portion of females have no yellow at all. These black females are Batesian mimics of a distasteful cousin, the Pipevine Swallowtail (*Battus philenor*). The difference is controlled by a single female-linked gene that suppresses an enzyme involved in the synthesis of the yellow pigment papiliochrome.

Batesian mimics need to be rare, and if only the females are mimics, they will be twice as rare. Müllerian mimic females may be more vulnerable than males as they seek out places to lay their eggs. Males, which may need to retain a distinctive color pattern to be recognized by a potential mate, may depend more on agility than on warning to escape their predators.

Mate recognition, however, may not be a problem for all mimics. In one Müllerian mimicry complex involving seven species of tropical American pierids (*Melinaea* spp.) and the longwing *Heliconius numata*, mate-seeking butterflies appear to be better than hungry birds at detecting the slight differences among its various members. In the eastern Andes, the nearly identical longwings *Heliconius melpomene amaryllis* and *H. timareta thelxinoe* rarely interbreed. Perhaps chemical signals or differing behavior keep the two apart.

Mimicry may involve behavior as well as appearance. The unpalatable Common Rose (*Pachlioptila aristolochiae*) flies slowly, with deeper wing-beats than some of its relatives. Female Common Mormons (*Papilio polytes*) both look and fly like the Common Rose, but male Common Mormons, which are not mimics, are rapid flyers.

A change in a single gene may be all that is necessary for mimicry to evolve. The "optix" gene controls the extreme variation in wing patterns of many species of *Heliconius*. A single optix mutation can change a *Heliconius* butterfly's entire appearance, swapping out one color pattern for another. If circumstances are right, it may become a successful mimic of a different species. *Heliconius melpomene* and *H. erato* probably arose on opposite sides of South America – *melpomene* in the east and *erato* in the west – during the late Pliocene, more than a million years ago. As they spread across the continent, they evolved forms with differing patterns and colors. Where they encountered each other, optix mutations brought each to mimic its opposite number. Coexisting pairs of *erato* and *melpomene* butterflies now look more like each other than like members of their own species elsewhere.

Some mimicry may be based not on toxins but on ability to escape capture. "Escape mimics" may copy other butterflies that are palatable but not worth chasing. Possible escape mimics in tropical America include the Dido Longwing (*Philaethria dido*), the Malachite (*Siproeta stelenes*), the Turquoise Emperor (*Doxocopa laurentia*) and butterflies in the genus *Prepona*. Not all butterfly experts, though, are convinced that such mimicry really exists, or that birds can remember difficult-to-catch species long enough to make escape mimicry evolutionarily worthwhile.

Finding a Mate

Most adult butterflies don't have long to live, so they must find mates quickly. Adult males are constantly on the prowl for females. They have two main ways of finding them: patrolling on the wing or waiting on a suitable perch for a prospective mate to fly by. Woodland and Rock Graylings (*Hipparchia fagi* and *H. hermione*) are perchers that will chase anything that moves, including a falling pinecone. Different species typically opt for either patrolling or perching and have evolved adaptations to match. Patrollers follow their larval host plants along forest tracks, looking for females seeking a place to lay their eggs. Larger and heavier butterflies tend to be perchers. Because they need rapid acceleration and high maneuverability to dash after their quarry, they tend to have high wing-loading and pointed wings.

Some butterflies patrol in warmer weather, when they can pick up more energy for flight, and perch during the cooler hours. A subordinate male, unable to drive a dominant male from a prime perching spot, may patrol until he can find an available perch. Speckled Woods (*Pararge aegeria*) studied in Sweden preferred to perch in sunlit forest glades. Males displaced from their perches spent 20 to 40 minutes on patrol before settling on a new perch in a smaller sunspot.

Many males defend territories around their perches. In eastern Asia, male Diana Foresters (*Lethe diana*) with territories are more strongly muscled than their rivals, aggressively chase off rivals, and get most of the matings. Many butterflies, metalmarks in particular, cluster their territories in communal assemblies, or leks, particularly near larval host plants where females are likely to emerge. Male Illioneus and Oileus Giant Owls (*Caligo illioneus* and *C. oileus*) establish leks along forest edges, where they chase off other males of their own and related species. Lekking allows males to concentrate their efforts and makes locating a male easier for females. If the lek has a supply of food, females may visit for nourishment rather than sex, and the males will be ready for them. In southeastern Brazil, male Phronius Satyrs (*Paryphthimoides phronius*) set up territories in sunny clearings. If fermenting fruit is available there they may defend it, but as females do not establish territories and males do not drive away intruding females, it seems that their territories are set up to attract mates rather than to preserve a food source for themselves.

Many butterflies, as humans do, increase their chances of finding a mate by heading for a place where the opposite sex is likely to congregate. "Hilltopping" males and virgin females follow the landscape upward, concentrating their numbers as they approach the summit. Hilltopping can be a particularly good strategy for rare, widely scattered butterflies, especially if available hilltops have enough flowers to feed their visitors. For more abundant species, which are able to meet more easily, the effort required to get to a hilltop might not be worth it.

Hilltopping male Desert Orangetips (*Anthocharis pima*) outrace each other to reach arriving females, a behavior called scramble completion polygyny. Other hilltoppers, including most swallowtails, set up territories. Some males switch between scrambling and defense over the course of the day, possibly in response to the number of other butterflies on the hilltop. Male Great Purple Hairstreaks (*Atlides halesus*) defend entire bushes on hilltops in Arizona. On one hilltop in western Brazil, territorial Thoas and Polydamas Swallowtails (*Papilio thoas* and *Battus polydamas*) and the kite swallowtail *Protesilaus orthosilaus* chased off rivals of all three species. In Africa, some populations of Common and Pierre's Acraeas (*Acraea encedon* and *A. encedana*) reverse their sexual roles. They have been infected by a bacterium, *Wolbachia*, that selectively kills males in the egg. Females establish hilltop territories and the few surviving males resort to them. In *Wolbachia*-free populations, as with other butterflies, males stake out the hilltops.

Butterfly Courtship

A great deal of butterfly courtship is little more than sexual harassment. A female can resist by assuming a refusal posture, raising her abdomen so that sexual contact becomes impossible. Once they have mated, female Ringlets (*Aphantopus hyperantus*) and Small Coppers (*Lycaena phlaeas*) fold their wings as males patrol nearby, probably to seek concealment. Female Small Coppers usually mate only once, so pursuit by other males does them no good.

Nonetheless, many males persist, often joined by other males. Male Squinting Bush Browns (*Bicyclus anynana*) can sometimes force reluctant females into multiple matings, but they are less successful at mating if another butterfly tries to interfere. Fending off unwanted males may keep females from feeding or laying their eggs. Harassing male Taylor's Checkerspots (*Euphydryas editha taylori*) drive egg-laying females to fly much farther than they would otherwise. Male Baltimore Checkerspots (*Euphydryas phaeton*), by contrast, tend to leave gravid females alone.

Some male *Heliconius* longwings are child molesters. In over 40% of *Heliconius* species, males hunt for female pupae on their larval food plants. They may home in on chemicals released by the chrysalis at the end of her development. Zebra Longwings (*H. charithonia*) also search by sight, focusing on plants that show larval damage. Individual males perch on and guard any female chrysalis they find, or groups of males may cluster around, waiting for the female to emerge. As soon as she appears, the males jostle each other for position, often copulating with her before she is completely out of her pupal skin. Other species do not wait even that long, breaking into the chrysalis and copulating with the female as soon as they can reach her genitalia. This seemingly abusive behavior may prevent copulation with extremely similar mimics. Where similar species occur together, one may be a pupa molester while the other may not; the difference may lower the likelihood of interspecific mistakes.

Other butterflies court their mates more graciously. A male Woodland Grayling (*Hipparchia fagi*) bows, flutters his wings and rotates his antennae as he attempts to induce a female to copulate. As he bows, he strokes her antennae with the androconial patches on his forewings,

adding the lure of pheromones to his display. The displays are slightly different in the related Rock Grayling (*H. hermione*), perhaps enough to prevent a female from mating with the wrong suitor.

Males of the Common Eggfly (*Hypolimnas bolina*) have large spots on each wing that reflect strongly in the ultraviolet range. These reflections are brightest when seen through a very narrow angle of view. Female eggflies are known to prefer males with brighter wing patches, and they respond more strongly to a flashing signal than to a steady display of color. Courting males make the most of this: they fly directly beneath the female, beating their wings 11 times per second through a shallow angle. From

***Danaus gilippus*, Rio Grande Valley, Texas, USA (Nymphalidae: Danaiinae)**
A courting male Queen (*Danaus gilippus*) releases pheromones near a female's antennae, causing her to land. He flutters around her until, if she is receptive, she folds her wings and he lands beside her. They mate and fly off, still joined together.

***Euphydryas editha taylori*,** **Willamette Valley, Oregon, USA (Lycaenidae: Lycaeninae)**
Taylor's Checkerspot (*Euphydryas editha taylori*) is an endangered butterfly of the Pacific Northwest, including southern British Columbia.
Males regularly harass gravid females, pursuing them for long distances even when they are trying to lay their eggs.

the female's point of view, all four wings flash ultraviolet at once, but only for that brief moment when the viewing angle is just right. The effect must be akin to a flashing strobe light and it may dazzle the female in the same way.

Pheromones are a crucial part of courtship. A male Squinting Bush Brown (*Bicyclus anynana*) wafts a mixture of three pheromones from the androconia on his wings. Females prefer older males, perhaps because they are proven survivors, and pheromone proportions can provide a female with information about the male's age. The androconia of courting male Green-veined Whites (*Pieris napi*) release an aphrodisiac compound called citral, synthesized from amino acids they took up as larvae. Citral may work because females respond to similar plant compounds when looking for a place to lay their eggs. But releasing citral takes its toll: virgin males live longer than courting males, even if the courting males do not mate.

If a male Oblong-spotted Birdwing (*Troides oblongomaculatus*) finds a free-flying female, he flutters around her in a series of circling loops, timing his last loop to

bring her antennae into contact with open scent pouches, filled with androconial scales, on the inner edges of his hindwings. With virgin females his efforts may succeed, but if she has mated before, the female resists by dropping to the ground. The male, undaunted, hovers over her, repeatedly beating her with his hindwings and showering her with scented scales from his androconia. This rarely works; after three or four attempts he usually gives up, and after a decent interval, the female flies off on her own.

Not all pheromones are sexual lures. During copulation some male butterflies transfer an antiaphrodisiac pheromone to the female that makes her less attractive to other males. This can have unwanted consequences. The antiaphrodisiac transferred by the male Large White (*Pieris brassicae*) repels males but attracts a tiny parasitic wasp that hitches a ride on the female and attacks her eggs after she has laid them. Fortunately, every time the female goes into a refusal posture she dissipates some of the pheromone, thereby not only avoiding a mating but reducing the risk of unwanted hitchhikers.

A copulating male delivers his sperm in a tough-walled package, called a spermatophore, that the female stores until she is ready to use it. In many butterflies the spermatophore carries a nuptial "gift": a rich supply of carbohydrates and proteins delivered in an ejaculate loaded with amino acids and other nitrogen-based nutrients. The ejaculate can also contain lipids, sugars, sterol, calcium phosphate and sodium and/or zinc. The female can use the gift for herself or for her eggs. Female swallowtails (*Papilio*), whites (*Pieris*) and longwings (*Heliconius*), among others, benefit from nuptial gifts.

Most male butterflies must build up their nuptial gifts as caterpillars. Except for the pollen-eating longwings, they cannot fully replenish their nutrient supplies after mating, even if they get some amino acids from nectar. Males that copulate more than once a day produce smaller amounts of ejaculate each time. Older male Diana Foresters (*Lethe diana*) have larger spermatophores than younger ones, perhaps because a younger male has more potential matings to look forward to and must save his limited resources for future opportunities.

Why does a male invest so much of himself in his ejaculate? The answer appears to be sperm competition. Though many female butterflies mate only once, other butterflies may copulate with several males, and usually most of a polyandrous female's eggs are fertilized by her last partner. A female Asian Swallowtail (*Papilio xuthus*) seems able to reject some or all of the sperm that have already penetrated her spermatheca, or sperm receptacle, in favor of those arriving from a new mating. Other butterflies may do the same. Having a particularly large and nutritious spermatophore apparently delays the moment when the female is ready to mate with another male; this increases the male's chances that it is his DNA that will go into his mate's eggs. Males also bulk up their spermatophores with infertile sperm, apparently to fill the female's reproductive organs and reduce her ability to accept sperm from another male.

Female Black-banded Hairstreaks (*Antigius attilia*) may mate four times every five days. Japanese researchers have found females with as many as 38 spermatophores in their bursa copulatrix, a spermatophore-holding chamber at the end of the oviduct. Female Green-veined Whites (*Pieris napi*) may mate up to six times. The nutrients they receive can extend their lifespan: polyandrous females live longer than females that mate only once, and they are more than half again as fecund.

Providing this gift is costly. A male's nuptial gifts can amount to 15% of his body mass. A single spermatophore from a male Green-veined White can provide enough nitrogen to supply 70 eggs. It can take a male Speckled Wood (*Pararge aegeria*) up to a week to build up a second, equally large spermatophore after his first mating. That's a long time for a butterfly that lives for 10 days or less as an adult.

The male Mountain White (*Leptophobia aripa elodia*) makes the smallest investment per spermatophore of any known butterfly. His first ejaculate is less than 1% of his body weight. Nonetheless, mating costs him a good deal. A study of Mountain Whites near Mexico City showed that virginal adult males, and males that mate only once, live about 12 days, while males that have sex more frequently die after a week or so. Oddly enough, this trade-off between sex and death does not always happen in more generous butterflies. Monarchs (*Danaus plexippus*) produce large and rich spermatophores but can mate multiple times with seemingly no effect on their lifespan. Monarchs are highly polyandrous and appear to be adapted to multiple matings, while Mountain Whites normally are not. Perhaps the Mountain White experimenters simply wore the poor creatures out.

Host Plants and Oviposition

Most butterflies oviposit (lay their eggs) on the host plants their caterpillars eat. However, there are exceptions. Female Marbled Whites (*Melanargia galathea*) drop their eggs in flight as they maneuver among tall grasses. Female Ringlets (*Aphantopus hyperantus*) perch on blades of grass to lay their eggs, but instead of attaching them to the vegetation they release them into the air, to land on the ground or the grass below.

Ovipositing female Baizana Clearwings (*Oleria baizana*) lay their eggs on the underside of a dead leaf in the litter beneath their host plant, a member of the nightshade family (Solanaceae). After they hatch, the caterpillars spend the day hiding in the leaf litter. A few hours before can affect her brood. In Britain, for example, Orange-tips (*Anthocharis cardamines*) reared on Cuckoo Flower (*Cardamine pratensis*) have smaller pupae, and males are smaller and emerge earlier, than those raised on Garlic Mustard (*Alliaria petiolata*). Large White (*Pieris brassicae*) caterpillars grow more slowly but end up weighing more on broccoli and cauliflower than they do on cabbage.

Some butterflies lay one egg at a time, while others lay many at once. Many butterflies that lay large clutches are unpalatable; a large cluster of eggs may be a warning. Pipevine Swallowtails (*Battus philenor*) pick up toxic alkaloids from Dutchman's pipe (*Aristolochia* spp.) and pass them on to their eggs. A study in Tennessee showed that predators – mostly crawling invertebrates – attacked larger swallowtail clutches less often than they did small ones, suggesting that a butterfly that lays toxic eggs is better off doing so in numbers.

Some butterflies oviposit on many types of plants, even if not all are ideal for their larvae. Old World Swallowtails (*Papilio machaon*) may oviposit on composites (Asteraceae) in North America and rues (Rutaceae) or carrot relatives (Apiaceae) in Europe. This can be a good strategy in a variable environment where the best plants are not always available, and it may make it harder for predators to find their broods by zeroing in on a specific plant.

Other butterflies are specialists. Some whites, including the Green-veined White (*Pieris napae*), lay exclusively on members of the cabbage family (Brassicaceae). Most gossamer-winged butterflies (Lycaenidae) use only one plant family or genus. Specialists may be better able to assimilate plant toxins. When caterpillars of 70 species of Costa Rican butterflies and moths were presented to predatory ants, the ants proved more likely to reject specialists that carried unpalatable chemicals from their hosts.

Common Longwings (*Heliconius erato*) lay their eggs on a number of passion vines (*Passiflora* spp.). Caterpillars grow larger and marginally faster on some passion vines than on others; the butterflies normally show a clear preference for the best species, even if others are easier to find. In Brazil's subtropical south, the butterflies are far less particular during the drier, cooler months, from July to December, when the quality of all passion vines declines.

Butterflies must choose the right individual plant and the right spot on the plant – not too sunny, so the egg

***Battus philenor*, Nashville, Tennessee, USA
(Papilionidae: Papilioninae)**

The Pipevine Swallowtail (*Battus philenor*) is one of a number of swallowtails that take up toxic chemicals from their host plants as caterpillars, and carry them in their bodies into adulthood. Other butterflies, including other swallowtails, mimic its appearance.

dawn they climb the plant, select a suitable leaf and systematically chew through its stalk. This takes them from about 20 minutes to a little over half an hour. As soon as they make the final cut, the leaf falls free and the caterpillar parachutes with it to the forest floor. There it remains for the day, hidden beneath the fallen leaf, which serves the caterpillar as both shelter and food.

Once a female finds a suitable plant, she lands and tests its surface with antennae, feet and ovipositor (the egg-laying organ), apparently looking for chemical confirmation that she has made the right choice. The choice development. The best spot for eggs may not be optimal for caterpillars. The amount of sun or shade matters, as does the orientation of the oviposition site to the sun. Fenton's Wood White (*Leptidea morsi*), a rare and declining butterfly from eastern Europe, avoids plants in full sun, preferring warm, shady spots oriented to the south and west. It prefers to lay near the top of the plant, where the air is warmer and fresh young leaves will be available for the hatchlings.

Finding the best spots takes energy and increases the risk of falling to a predator. Another butterfly may have gotten there first. Some butterflies use the presence of others as a timesaving cue for finding host plants, and Green-veined Whites prefer plants already carrying eggs from other females. Nonetheless, if eggs or caterpillars are already on the plant, it may be better to go elsewhere.

Butterflies can adapt to new host plants, with varying results. The Sweet Potato Butterfly (*Acraea acerata*) is a major pest of sweet potatoes, an important crop in many African countries that was imported from the Americas during colonial times. Before its introduction, the caterpillars fed on native plants in the same genus (*Ipomoea*). They still do, but have also switched over enthusiastically to the new arrival. The butterfly's larvae survive better and its female pupae grow larger on sweet potatoes than they do on their original native diet.

Ardys and Tulcis Crescents (*Anthanassa ardys* and *A. tulcis*) in Monteverde, Costa Rica, lay eggs on plants in the family Acanthaceae. Most are fine for their caterpillars, but they sometimes select an African species introduced in the mid-20th century. If they do, their young cannot eat it and will die. These butterflies apparently have not had time to adapt to the deadly new arrival.

Caterpillars of the Richmond Birdwing (*Ornithoptera richmondia*) of east central Australia feed on leaves of Dutchman's pipe (Aristolochiaceae). Ovipositing females choose plants by picking up chemical signals with receptors on their forelegs. Unfortunately, South American Dutchman's pipes cultivated in Australian gardens pro-

Social Caterpillars, Cannibals and Myrmecophiles

All the growth a butterfly undergoes, in terms of mass, it does as a caterpillar. How long a caterpillar takes to grow depends on a number of things, but the quality and quantity of its food are probably the most important. Caterpillars that eat grass, for example, tend to be small and to grow slowly for their size. Large caterpillars may grow surprisingly quickly, perhaps to get past a stage when they are particularly conspicuous to predators.

The first thing a caterpillar eats is usually its own eggshell. In Pierre's Acraea (*Acraea encedana*), an African butterfly that lays in clutches of a hundred or so, its next meal may be the unhatched eggs of its siblings. Caterpillar cannibalism is not uncommon. Common Longwing caterpillars (*Heliconius erato*) eat eggs and young caterpillars of their own kind but appear able to recognize and, to some extent, avoid the eggs of their siblings.

***Feniseca tarquinius*, St. John's Conservation Area, Ontario, Canada (Lycaenidae: Miletinae)**

Caterpillars of the Harvester (*Feniseca tarquinius*) feed on aphids, and their carnivorous diet helps them grow quickly. They can mature in as few as eight days, molting only four times – one less than in most other butterflies.

Most, but not all, butterfly caterpillars eat leaves. There are also flower-eating caterpillars, such as those of some tropical American hairstreaks (*Parrhasius* spp.), and carnivores, like the caterpillar of the North American Harvester (*Feniseca tarquinius*), which lives entirely on aphids. The caterpillar of the Moth butterfly (*Liphyra brassolis*) of Asia and Australia lives in the nests of Weaver ants (*Oecophylla smaragdina*) and dines on their larvae; the adult's mouthparts are functionless and it does not feed at all. Britain's smallest butterfly, the Small Blue (*Cupido minimus*), lays its eggs in the flower heads of Kidney Vetch (*Anthyllis vulneraria*). Its caterpillars eat the flowers, the developing seeds and any smaller caterpillars that pass by.

pheromone is there. In the mountains of Mexico, broods of 200 or more caterpillars of the Social White (*Eucheira socialis*) build a watertight communal nest with tough walls of silk. The caterpillars feed at night, following pheromone-marked silken trails they lay through the foliage, and rest together in the nest during the day. The colony even pupates in the nest, and emerges together as adults.

Broods of about 100 Glanville Fritillary caterpillars (*Melitaea cinxia*) weave a web over their host plant and feed and bask within it. As a warm caterpillar is more active and can feed more rapidly, basking is important, especially at the northern end of its range in Finland. The caterpillars are black with bright red heads, and even at air temperatures of 10°C (50°F) basking broods can raise their body temperatures above 30°C (86°F).

After feeding on their host plant for 10 to 15 days, Eurasian blue caterpillars (*Phengaris* spp.) drop to the ground. There they are found and adopted by *Myrmica* ants. The ants carry the caterpillars into their nest, where they live, protected from their enemies, for up to two years before pupating. Some, like the Alcon Blue (*P. alcon*), are fed by the attending workers, while others, including the Scarce Large Blue (*P. teleius*), eat the ants' brood.

More than half of all gossamer-wings (Lycaenidae) and about a third of the metalmarks (Riodinidae) live in a relationship with ants, one that is either mutually beneficial or parasitic. The term for such a relationship is myrmecophily, from the Greek word for ant, *myrmex*. Some myrmecophiles are facultative, or able to get along without ants if necessary, but there are many obligate myrmecophiles that must interact with ants – and often with specific ant genera – to survive.

Myrmecophilous caterpillars draw ants into these seemingly one-sided relationships with specialized structures called ant organs. Tentacle organs on the thorax or abdomen release pheromones that lure the ants and suppress their aggressive instincts. Sound-producing organs create vibrations that (we think) attract ants. In

hat the ants harvest. The droplets presumably provide
he benefit that leads ants to tolerate the caterpillars in
he first place. In metalmarks, a set of inflated bristles on
he thorax, called balloon setae, may – although this is far
rom clear – release a pheromone that summons the ants
o the caterpillar's defense.

Producing nectar for ants can have other advantages.
Some tropical Asian oakblue caterpillars (*Arhopala* spp.)
eed on leaves of *Macaranga* trees that are protected by
stinging ants (*Crematogaster* spp.) living in their hollow
stems. Supplying these ant guards with nectar keeps the
caterpillars from being attacked. The ants have been in a
relationship with the trees for between 16 and 20 million
years. About 8 million years ago, tiny scale insects got
nvolved, providing the ants with sweet secretions while
he ants guarded them. The oakblues appear to have
horned in on this arrangement about 2 million years ago,
aking rapid advantage of a symbiotic relationship that
already existed.

Development and Diapause

Many butterflies develop on a fast track, passing from
egg to adult in days or weeks. They are often multivol-
ine, meaning that they produce several generations in

this point is fast approaching. Cooler temperatures slow down a caterpillar's development, reducing its chances of completing its growth before the critical point arrives. The host plant can make a difference too. Wood Whites (*Leptidea sinapis*) in southern Sweden tend to enter diapause if they live in forests but develop directly in meadows, where temperatures are warmer. This is not just a response to temperature. Under similar conditions, caterpillars raised on Bitter Vetch (*Lathyrus linifolius*), their usual forest host plant, were more likely to enter diapause than those raised on Meadow Pea (*L. pratensis*), their normal food in meadows. Caterpillars of the very similar Réal's Wood White (*Leptidea reali*), a meadow specialist, rarely get to eat Bitter Vetch, and they enter diapause less often than their near relatives. They do not seem to be influenced by their host plant; in a study, rearing them on Bitter Vetch made no difference.

Before a butterfly, in whatever stage, overwinters it has to find shelter. Caterpillars, with their ability to spin silk, can construct shelters of their own. Unlike many moths, though, they do not spin dense, thick-walled

cocoons. The Poplar Admiral (*Limenitis populi*) hibernate in a refuge, or hibernaculum, that it constructs out of a fresh leaf as early as late July. First it attaches an edge of the leaf to a twig with strands of silk. Next, it cuts the attached portion free and folds the leaf around itself. Before it enters its winter sleep, it uses more silk to seal its rolled-up enclosure and to fix the completed hibernaculum lengthwise along the twig.

Butterflies, Nectar and Pollen

The adult butterfly's task is to mate and lay eggs. The bulk of its diet, whether from flowers or rotting fruit, is sugar. Floral sugars vary in both chemistry and concentration. Swallowtails and whites prefer nectars that are rich in sucrose, a complex sugar, over those rich in simple sugars such as glucose and fructose, but in other butterflies there may be no clear preference. Nectar contains other things water, minerals and amino acids, which adult butterflies can use as a source of nitrogen for nuptial gifts, egg production and general fitness. Glasswings (Ithomiini) visit flowers whose nectars contain toxins that the butterflies use for defense.

Butterflies take nectar from a wide range of flow-

lycisca) prefers to visit the long, tubular flowers of a ginger relative, *Calathea crotalifera* (Family Marantaceae), but does not trigger the flower's specialized pollinating mechanism. Rather than being pollinators, *Eurybia* butterflies are nectar thieves.

Sugars provide butterflies with energy, but most butterflies have already taken up (as caterpillars) most or all of the protein they will need to produce sperm and eggs. That arrangement usually makes for long-lived caterpillars and – hibernation aside – short-lived adults. Tropical American longwings (*Heliconius*) are an exception. Longwings visit flowers, including gourd flowers (Cucurbitaceae), for nectar and for pollen, which contains far higher amounts of amino acids than nectar. Longwings cannot eat the pollen grains, so they store them on the outside of the proboscis. They process the grains as they roost, often overnight, by repeatedly coiling and uncoiling the proboscis while soaking them in a saliva-like fluid. This behavior, which may have evolved from proboscis-cleaning activities in other butterflies, breaks up the grains and releases their contents. The butterflies drink the resulting liquid with its amino acids and discard the empty shells. The amino acids will produce 80% of the protein that goes into their eggs. Longwing caterpillars thus do not need to store protein for later egg production and can grow more quickly. Feeding on pollen may also extend the adults' lives. Adult *Heliconius* butterflies can live up to eight months; they spread their egg-laying over their lifetime rather than, as most butterflies do, manufacturing eggs from protein they took in as larvae and depositing them soon after emerging as adults.

Pollen plants and their *Heliconius* butterflies appear to have evolved together, and the butterflies are the plants' chief pollinators. Having the right pollen plants in the area is an essential for a female *Heliconius* looking for a good spot to lay her eggs. She will use their presence as a site marker even if the passion-vine leaves its larvae will eat are not ready. Being long-lived means that she can afford to wait for them to grow before ovipositing, as long as the pollen she needs is available.

Butterfly Migration

The migrations of the Monarch butterfly (*Danaus plexippus*) are world-famous, but other butterflies, including whites, sulphurs and swallowtails, are also accomplished long-distance migrants. Large numbers of Gulf Fritillaries (*Agraulis vanillae*) migrate through the Florida peninsula in late summer and fall. They return northward during the spring and much of the summer, depositing eggs as they go. At the other end of their range, butterflies in Tucumán, Argentina, have been seen migrating to the east.

Painted Ladies (*Vanessa cardui*) migrate in both North America and Europe, where they cross the Mediterranean with the help of tailwinds from North Africa. During an enormous European migration in 2009 they reached northern Norway, 6,500 km (4,040 mi) from their southernmost wintering areas. Some two million butterflies

***Danaus plexippus*, Wisconsin, USA (Nymphalidae: Danaiinae)**
Once this Monarch butterfly (*Danaus plexippus*) emerges from its chrysalis, and after its wings expand and dry, it may be ready to join one of the greatest animal migrations on the planet. Butterflies from Wisconsin will join other eastern Monarchs, flying southward toward the mountains of Mexico.

were radar-tracked crossing 300 km (190 mi) of the English coastline during two days in May. No one butterfly makes the full trip. Adult Painted Ladies live only a few weeks, and it may take six generations of butterflies, hatched at different points along the route, to complete the migratory cycle.

Tropical butterflies may migrate as well. At the onset of the dry season, more than half of the butterflies in the dry forests of northwestern Costa Rica leave for humid areas elsewhere. At least 10 species of butterfly have been recorded crossing Gatún Lake in Panama at the onset of the rainy season. Statira Sulphurs (*Aphrissa statira*) and Many-banded Daggerwings (*Marpesia chiron*) cross in numbers in May and June. They are able to compensate for wind drift and are clearly heading in a specific direction.

Monarch butterfly migrations once involved at least a billion butterflies per year – the greatest movements of land animals on Earth. Although their numbers are sadly diminished, their journeys remain a wonder of the animal world. Monarchs in eastern North America take at least three generations to complete their annual migratory cycle. Northern migrants fly southward to their wintering grounds in central Mexico (a few end up in Florida or Cuba instead) and start northward again in the following spring, but only about one-tenth live to return. Most get no farther than the southern or central United States, laying eggs on southern milkweeds before they die. In less than a month their offspring resume the journey north. They give rise to at least one more generation before the butterflies at last reach the northern limit of their range.

Monarchs cannot tolerate freezing temperatures. Though they probably evolved as migrants, only northern populations need to migrate. Southern populations, from Florida through Mexico and the West Indies to northern South America, are residents. They have shorter and more rounded wings than their far-traveling cousins, but being a migrant requires more than larger wings. Migratory butterflies such as the Red Admiral (*Vanessa atalanta*) have high concentrations of mitochondria in their flight muscles, increasing their ability to metabolize oxygen. The Monarch's adaptations for migration go deep into its genetic makeup, affecting not only flying ability and stamina but also endocrine "switches" that trigger the migratory impulse as days grow shorter in fall and longer in spring, and the neurological and sensory wiring that enables the butterfly to pick up the cues it needs to find its way.

How Monarchs do find their way has only recently been worked out. As they fly southward, an internal compass, located in a dense central complex in the brain, reacts to visual information about the sun's position and the patterns of polarized light in the sky. A clock based on proteins in their antennae – it works even if one antenna is missing – adjusts for the time of day as the sun's position changes. The combined information from compass and clock keeps the butterflies headed in the right direction. Another, recently discovered compass in the antennae tracks their path against Earth's magnetic field; it probably keeps them on track on cloudy days.

The Monarch's orientation system is not entirely foolproof. The magnetic compass works only if it is triggered by the right wavelengths of blue to ultraviolet light. If they can see the sun, the butterflies ignore information from the magnetic compass even if they need it. When experimenters shifted butterflies 2,500 km (1,550 mi) to the west, they followed their usual southwesterly course, unable to correct their path. This suggests that Monarchs rely on compasses for navigation but may lack a full-time internal positioning system that can tell them where they are. Still, this is a sophisticated mechanism for such a tiny-brained creature. The eastern Monarchs' wintering areas in Mexico are small, and without precise guidance they would be hard to find. Other butterflies' orientation systems may be simpler; Painted Ladies, for example, appear to lack the antennal clock.

To find their way north again, Monarchs need to reset their sun compass. The temperatures in the eastern Monarch's winter quarters in the mountains of Mexico drop close to freezing in January. As the butterflies begin to grow dormant in the cold, the low temperature stimulates their compass to switch direction. The timing of the process allows the returning butterflies to reach their breeding grounds in the southern United States just as new milkweed plants are sprouting. The Monarchs' entire, vast journey may have evolved to match the presence and availability of milkweeds at different points along their route.

Butterflies Under Threat

Over the past 20 years the number of eastern North American Monarchs (*Danaus plexippus*) wintering in Mexico has fallen from more than a billion to 56.5 million in 2014, a decline of over 90%. Smaller populations west of the Rockies have fallen by half. In August 2014 the Center for Biological Diversity, the Center for Food Safety, the Xerces Society and long-time Monarch expert Dr. Lincoln Brower petitioned the US Fish and Wildlife Service (FWS) to list the Monarch butterfly as threatened under the Endangered Species Act. In December 2014 the FWS agreed that the petition contained "substantial information indicating that listing may be warranted" and announced the launch of a status review, the first step toward a possible listing.

For many years we assumed that the biggest threat to the Monarch was degradation of the Mexican oyamel fir, pine and oak forests where the eastern population winters. But the chief culprit may be closer to hand.

Milkweeds, their larval food plant, have been eradicated from much of the American Midwest. Vast fields of genetically modified herbicide- and pesticide-resistant crops – particularly corn, soybeans and cotton resistant to the herbicide glyphosate – are sprayed with chemicals that destroy milkweeds and kill off the butterflies. In early 2014 the National Resources Defense Council (NRDC) petitioned the US Environmental Protection Agency (EPA) to reexamine its approval of glyphosate. When the EPA did not respond, NRDC filed a lawsuit in February 2015 to compel them to act.

The plight of the Monarch has brought butterfly conservation to the front pages, and it's none too soon. Butterflies are disappearing in many parts of the world. Populations are in decline and communities are losing species in the Central Valley of California, in Britain, in the grasslands of central Europe, and undoubtedly in many other places that have yet to be surveyed. Seventy-one percent of British butterflies have lost ground since 1970. In the 20th century the Netherlands lost 24% of

Glaucopsyche xerces (extinct), Florida Museum of Natural History, Gainesville, Florida, USA
(Lycaenidae: Polyommatinae)
The Xerces Blue (*Glaucopsyche xerces*) was the first known butterfly in North America to be exterminated by human activity. Found only around sand dunes near San Francisco, it disappeared in the 1940s as urban development swallowed its habitat.

its butterfly species, Britain lost 9%, and Moravia (in the Czech Republic) 60%. Fifteen percent of Japan's butterflies are now endangered, and some grassland species have lost over 95% of their population.

These figures are for temperate-zone butterflies. For the tropics, where 90% of the world's butterflies live, almost no comparable information is available. The information we have on conserving and managing temperate butterflies may not apply in the tropics, so a realistic list of globally endangered butterflies does not exist. The IUCN Red List, which categorizes threat for species worldwide, had assessed only 683 species of butterfly by the end of 2014 – less than 4% of the total – and many of those assessments were more than 10 years out-of-date.

The highly urbanized island of Singapore has lost 38% of its butterfly species, but in most cases, what our rampant destruction of tropical forests is doing we do not know. Almost all of the 972 butterflies known from West African rainforests between Senegal and Togo were still there in 2006, though 87% of the forest itself has been lost – grounds for pride but hardly for complacency. If the surviving forest, now largely in protected areas, is lost, that picture could change drastically.

Trade in rare butterflies, often captured illegally, reportedly brings in US$200 million per year. All of the birdwings (*Ornithoptera*, *Trogonoptera* and *Troides* spp.), *Bhutanitis* and *Teinopalpa* swallowtails, and a few others, including the Apollo (*Parnassius apollo*), are listed under the Convention on International Trade in Endangered Species of Wild Fauna and Flora (CITES) and can be traded internationally only under its provisions. Three species – the Homerus Swallowtail (*Papilio homerus*) of Jamaica, the Luzon Peacock Swallowtail (*Papilio chikae*) of the Philippines, and Queen Alexandra's Birdwing (*Ornithoptera alexandrae*) of New Guinea – are listed in CITES Appendix I; this means that international commercial trade in these butterflies (with certain narrow exceptions) is banned. Hisayoshi Kojima, a Japanese dealer with worldwide connections, was arrested for smuggling endangered butterflies, including Appendix I species, after a US Fish and Wildlife Service sting operation in 2006. He was sentenced to 21 months in prison and a fine of US$38,731. The story of his arrest is told in Jessica Speart's book *Winged Obsession*.

Far more butterflies are threatened by habitat loss, including loss of their host plants, than by direct exploitation. Grassland butterflies have been hard-hit in temperate regions. In tropical areas such as Southeast Asia, primary-forest butterflies are probably at the greatest risk, particularly on islands such as Sulawesi, where 43% of the butterfly species are found nowhere else. The more specific a butterfly's requirements and the more local its distribution, the more likely it is to disappear. A 2010 study in Catalonia, Spain, showed that butterfly communities were becoming more and more dominated by common generalist species, particularly in grasslands and Mediterranean scrub.

Mowing, overgrazing and the use of herbicides and pesticides degrade butterfly habitat. Logging and conversion for agriculture destroy tropical forests. Commercial tree plantations, farming and urban development replace natural prairies and meadows. Invasive alien plants crowd out natural hosts for caterpillars, though butterflies do sometimes adapt to them. Taylor's Checkerspot (*Euphydryas editha taylori*), an endangered North American butterfly, now depends entirely on Ribwort Plantain (*Plantago lanceolata*), an alien. An invasive parasitic fly, *Sturmia bella*, has been implicated in the decline of the Small Tortoiseshell (*Aglais urticae*) in Britain. Even recreational activities can be a problem. Visitors to the Indiana Dunes National Lakeshore on Lake Michigan flush butterflies and may be reducing the egg-laying success of the endangered Karner Blue (*Lycaeides melissa samuelis*).

Butterflies and Climate Change

Looming over everything else is the threat of climate change. Its effect on butterflies, at least so far, has been ambiguous. Rising temperatures in the alpine zone of the Colorado Rockies may make it harder for the eggs of mountain butterflies to survive, but a longer warm season may give the adults extra time to fly, mate and lay more eggs. Some butterflies may increase their numbers and ranges as temperatures rise. Southern grassland butterflies, for example, have increased in Korea. The Tawny Coster (*Acraea terpsicore*), a rapidly spreading Asian immigrant first recorded in Australia in 2012 and already established, may spread more widely there as climate change creates new areas favorable to it.

In Europe and North America, southern species have shifted north. Butterflies such as the Arran Brown (*Erebia ligea*) and Common Blue (*Polyommatus icarus*) have now colonized Padjelanta National Park, just below the Arctic Circle in northern Sweden. In southeastern Manitoba, Canada, the Common Buckeye (*Junonia coena*) has expanded its range northward by 150 km (95 mi) since the 1970s and the Baltimore Checkerspot (*Euphydryas phaeton*) by 70 km (45 mi). Many temperate butterflies are now flying earlier in the year, particularly in spring. Most Swedish butterflies are flying earlier in spring than they were a few decades ago, and some late-appearing species are active later in the season. The average shift forward has been just under four days for each 1°C (1.8°F) rise in temperature. An average shift of 2.4 days per degree Celsius has been predicted for many, if not most, Canadian butterflies.

The long-term effects of climate change, however, may be disastrous for many butterflies. Tropical butterflies may already be near the upper limits of tolerable temperature. Higher temperatures have been shown to suppress immune response in the Squinting Bush Brown (*Bicyclus anynana*). Warmer temperatures are known to reduce the survival of overwintering larvae of the Woodland Ringlet (*Erebia medusa*). Even butterflies that gain new territory at the cooler edge of their range may lose ground in warmer areas.

Climate change may worsen the effects of habitat fragmentation and loss. Fragmentation can trap butterflies in patches of habitat that become steadily less suitable for them as the climate shifts. Butterflies driven out of their habitats by changing temperatures may find fewer new areas to colonize. In Britain, 20 out of 27 butterflies lost range between 1997 and 2007 as their habitats degraded, despite expansions into new habitat in warm years. With climate change, butterfly species are expected to decline markedly in Britain, even though there may be more individual butterflies as common species increase. One model predicted that by 2080 nearly half of the butterflies in areas counted by the UK Butterfly Monitoring Scheme would be individuals of a single species, the Meadow Brown (*Maniola jurtina*).

In Europe, northern species are more vulnerable than species adapted to warmer temperatures. Climate change is a particular threat to alpine and arctic butterflies, which are adapted to colder habitats that will shrink and deteriorate as warming temperatures move farther north and higher up the mountains. Butterflies isolated on mountain peaks, including local, genetically distinct populations of the Yellow-spotted Ringlet (*Erebia manto*) in central Europe, could be squeezed out of existence as warming temperatures force them into ever smaller areas. The Apollo (*Parnassius apollo*), a flagship species for conservation in Europe, is already extinct in three of its range countries and is diminishing in 12 others. Its meadow habitats are being replaced with farmland and planted forest, and it is particularly vulnerable to climate change.

Parnassius smintheus, **Colorado, USA**
(Papilionidae: Parnassiinae)
The Rocky Mountain Parnassian (*Parnassius smintheus*) is a high-mountain butterfly ranging through the Rockies from southern Alaska to New Mexico. Climate change is predicted to affect it throughout its range, and may lead to the extinction of local populations.

Conserving Butterflies

Broader environmental issues aside, conserving butterflies at a local level means conserving larval host plants and, for flower-feeding butterflies, adult nectar sources. It means knowing their requirements for courtship and mating and understanding their relationships with predators, parasites and (for myrmecophiles) attending ants. In the American Midwest, tall-grass prairie butterflies are declining even in well-managed reserves. To conserve such species, we need to know – in detail – what each requires, and manage their habitats accordingly.

Restoring butterfly habitat may be crucial for butterflies with few natural refuges left. In the Pacific Northwest, Fender's Blue (*Icaricia icarioides fenderi*) depends on prairie-oak ecosystems rich in lupines (*Lupinus* spp.), its larval host plant. Its entire range covers only about 185 hectares (460 acres). Its habitat is intensely managed, and new areas are being restored and planted with lupines. Butterflies are breeding in the restored areas, but in only about half the numbers found in the original habitat. Much more needs to be done.

Butterflies may not need vast spaces in which to recover. In Switzerland, strips or patches of land of less than half a hectare (1.2 acres) sown with a mixture of wildflowers, attracted two-thirds of the butterfly species in the area and provided food for a number of their caterpillars. Though restored habitats are most valuable if they are close to existing forest or grassland reserves, studies in the Netherlands show that even vacant lots and rooftop gardens can provide potential habitat for rare butterflies.

And damage can be undone. Mauritius, in the Indian Ocean, may have lost three species of butterflies found nowhere else as alien plants invaded forests and crowded out native plants. Where woody weeds have been removed, the surviving forest butterflies have recovered their numbers. In northeastern Georgia, United States, woodland butterfly communities rebounded after the removal of invasive Chinese Privet (*Ligustrum sinense*). In Ghana's Kakum Forest, forest butterfly communities showed signs of recovery in abandoned plantations only nine years after they were replanted with native trees.

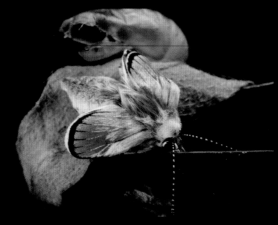

Individual species can also be restored. The Marsh Fritillary (*Euphydryas aurinia*) was successfully reintroduced to northern England in 2007, using captive-bred caterpillars from the last surviving local population plus extra larvae from western Scotland. The Large Blue (*Phengaris arion*) became extinct in Britain in 1979, just as scientists were realizing that its caterpillars feed on the larvae of a single species of grassland ant, *Myrmica sabulati*, and the butterfly cannot survive without it. It has been reestablished using butterflies from Sweden and is now doing well in areas managed to preserve the short-grass habitat required by the ant. It has even been suggested that the vanished Xerces Blue (*Glaucopsyche xerces*) of California, not seen since the 1940s, could be a candidate for high-tech "De-Extinction" through cloning.

Farming butterflies to provide specimens for collectors and exhibits for butterfly houses has been promoted as a way to promote sustainable livelihoods in developing countries. In the East Usumbara Mountains of Tanzania the Amani Butterfly Project provides roughly US$200 per year for 350 households. Fifty-five percent of the farmers are women. Butterflies taken from the forest are reared to provide cocoons for overseas sale and for breeding stock; their host plants are grown in home gardens. Birdwings have been farmed in Papua New Guinea under the Insect Farming and Trading Agency (IFTA) since 1978, based on planting *Aristolochia* vines, which wild butterflies adopt as food plants. However, overall payments have decreased and few farmers stay in the business for long. The IFTA's value to conservation remains, at best, unproven.

Butterfly farming can have unplanned-for results. Since 2007 the Julia Heliconian (*Dryas iulia*) has become an invasive alien in southern Thailand, reaching Langkawi Island, off northwestern Peninsular Malaysia, in 2009. The invaders presumably derived from butterflies bred at the Phuket Butterfly Garden for release at weddings and Buddhist ceremonies.

We need to know more and to do better. In many parts of the world, butterflies are disappearing at a rapid rate. We need to understand what is happening to them, and why, if we are to stop or reverse their decline. We need to create space for butterflies.

If you are interested enough to be reading this book, you can help. Citizen science projects in North America – including Monarch Watch, the Western Monarch Count, the Vanessa Migration Project, and the Los Angeles Butterfly Survey – welcome volunteers. In Britain you can contribute to the Butterflies for the New Millennium Project and the United Kingdom Butterfly Monitoring Scheme (UKBMS). There are similar projects around the world, and organizations such as the Xerces Society that deserve your support.

Your yard can become a butterfly garden. Monarch Watch sells seed kits, containing milkweeds and other plants appropriate for your region, that you can use to create a Monarch way station. It can be at your home, your school or anywhere else where you have permission to plant. You can even certify your way station as part of an international network of Monarch refuges. Butterfly conservation is important, and you can be part of it.

Lycaeides melissa samuelis, Toledo, Ohio, USA (Lycaenidae: Polyommatinae)

The endangered Karner Blue (*Lycaeides melissa samuelis*) vanished from much of northeastern North America as its pine barrens habitat succumbed to development. Today it is a flagship species, a symbol for conservation not just of butterflies but of the ecosystems where they live.

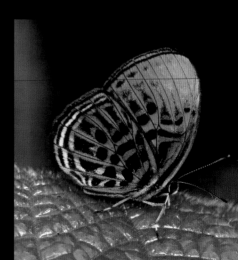

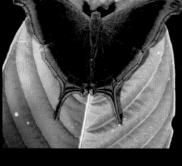

For many people, swallowtails are the quintessential butterflies: large, showy, easy to spot and a pleasure to watch. Not every swallowtail, though, has the extended "tails" on the hindwings that give the family its English name. The swallowtail family is a small one as butterfly families go, with only about 600 species worldwide. Its greatest numbers are found in the Old World, especially in the Indo-Australian region, home to almost half of the family (about 260 species).

Swallowtails include the largest of all butterflies. A female Queen Alexandra's Birdwing (*Ornithoptera alexandrae*), a highly localized and Endangered species from Papua New Guinea, can stretch to more than 28 cm (11 in) from wingtip to wingtip. The long, narrow wings of the male African Giant Swallowtail (*Papilio antimachus*) may reach 25 cm (9.8 in) across. At up to 20 cm (8 in) across, the Homerus Swallowtail (*Papilio homerus*), an Endangered species confined to the mountains of Jamaica, is the largest butterfly in the New World.

Swallowtails are powerful, often heavy-bodied fliers capable of traveling long distances, and several are migratory. When taking nectar, swallowtails often flutter in the air rather than landing, to keep their size and weight from dragging down the flowers they visit. Many swallowtails are highly convincing mimics, either of other swallowtails or of butterflies from other families.

With one exception, all swallowtails are divided into two subfamilies: the apollos and festoons (Parnassiinae) and the "typical" swallowtails (Papilioninae). The Archaic Swallowtail or Short-horned Baronia (*Baronia brevicornis*) is the only member of the subfamily Baroniinae. A tailless dark brown insect variably patterned in yellowish white or, in some females, orange, it resembles some early fossil butterflies. *Baronia* may be the last relic of an ancient – if not the oldest living – butterfly lineage. It lives in the dry tropical forests of southwestern Mexico, where its larvae feed on *Acacia* leaves, the only swallowtail caterpillars to do so regularly.

▶ *Papilio machaon*, Switzerland
Papilio machaon, "the" Swallowtail. See page 45.

The apollos and festoons probably arose in central Asia. Molecular evidence suggests that they diversified some 42 to 65 million years ago, when India collided with the Asian mainland, pushing up the Himalayas and the Tibetan plateau. Today they are found mostly at high elevations. The subfamily ranges across temperate Europe and Asia, reaching its highest diversity in the Himalayas. Only five species in one genus, *Parnassius*, have reached North America, where they range through the western mountains from Alaska to New Mexico.

Most parnassians lack tails. However, the luehdorfias (*Luehdorfia* spp.) of eastern Asia have a pair of tails, members of the Asian genus *Sericinus* have particularly long ones, and the extravagant, rare and much sought-after Himalayan and Chinese butterflies of the genus *Bhutanitis* sport three or four pairs each.

▶ *Parnassius apollo*, Switzerland

The Apollo (*Parnassius apollo*) is at home on steep slopes and flower-covered alpine meadows, where adults visit thistles and knapweeds (*Centaurea*) and lay their eggs on succulent stonecrops (*Sedum*). Females may reach 9 cm (3.5 in) across. Local populations of Apollos are scattered across the mountainous regions of Europe and temperate Asia, mostly at elevations between 500 and 2,400 m (1,640–7,900 ft). Males visit tall, long-stemmed flowers while females keep close to the ground, apparently to avoid pursuit by their mates.

▶▶ *Zerynthia polyxena*, Padan Plain, Italy

The Southern Festoon (*Zerynthia polyxena*) frequents sunny Mediterranean slopes, mostly below 900 m (3,000 ft), from southern France to the Ural Mountains. It flies in a single brood from April to June. Adults are usually on the wing for only three weeks. Festoon caterpillars feed on birthworts (*Aristolochia*), and the toxins in their food plants pass from the caterpillars to the adults. The blue and red spots on the Southern Festoon's hindwings may be a warning to predators that this is a butterfly to avoid.

BIRDWINGS

Ornithoptera, Troides and *Trogonoptera*

Alfred Russel Wallace called birdwings "the largest, the most perfect, and the most beautiful of butterflies." When he caught his first Golden Birdwing (*Ornithoptera croesus*), "the finest butterfly in the world," in the Moluccas in 1859, "I was nearer fainting with delight and excitement than I have ever been in my life; my heart beat violently, and the blood rushed to my head, leaving a headache for the rest of the day." Birdwings have been objects of desire ever since. Tens of thousands have been exported from butterfly ranches in Indonesia, Papua New Guinea and neighboring countries since the 1980s. Pairs of Queen Alexandra's Birdwing, the largest butterfly in the world, have been smuggled out of New Guinea and offered for sale for more than US$8,500.

▲ ▶ *Ornithoptera priamus*, Lae, Papua New Guinea
The Common Green or Cairns Birdwing (*Ornithoptera priamus*) is the best-known and one of the most widely distributed of the 36 birdwing species. It ranges from the Moluccas through New Guinea to the Solomon Islands and northeast Queensland, Australia. This is a male. Females are dark brown, marked with white, and are larger than the males at 22 cm (8.5 in) across.

◀ *Troides oblongomaculatus*, Lae,
Papua New Guinea

The 21 *Troides* birdwings, patterned in black and irides
golden yellow, live in rainforests from Sri Lanka to New
The Oblong-spotted Birdwing (*Troides oblongomaculat*
Guinea is their easternmost representative. Like the C
Green Birdwing, it is widely raised for export on butte
ranches, where males copulate with unresisting femal
as they emerge from their chrysalises.

▼ *Trogonoptera brookiana*, Cameron Highla
West Malaysia

Wallace named this "magnificent insect" in 1855 after Ja
Brooke, first of the White Rajahs of Sarawak. Today Raja
Birdwing (*Trogonoptera brookiana*), which can measure
cm (6.7 in) across, is a symbol of this Malaysian state. It
throughout Borneo, Sumatra and the Malay Peninsula r
peninsular Thailand. Females spend their lives in the tre
are rarely seen, but the males often fly low or settle, sor
numbers, at sulfur springs and mineral seeps. Urine-so
attracts them too (I can vouch for this personally).

◄ *Pachliopta aristolochiae*, Erawan National Park, Thailand

The Common Rose (*Pachlioptila aristolochiae*), a widespread and variable Southeast Asian butterfly, ranges from India and China to Bali and the Philippines. Its caterpillars feed largely on Dutchman's pipe (*Aristolochia* spp). The toxins they pick up from their diet make this species and its near relatives highly unpalatable to birds. A number of other swallowtails mimic them, copying both their appearance and their manner of flight. One form of the female Common Mormon (*Papilio polytes*) mimics the Common Rose but lacks red on its body.

◄ *Papilio paris*, Khao Yai National Park Thailand

The 25 species (and more than 100 subspecies) of peacock swallowtails (subgenus *Achillides*) are elegant black butterflies; most of the males are variously patched or banded with the iridescent blues and greens of a peacock's train. They range from India, Japan and the Russian Far East to tropical northern Australia. The Paris Peacock or Paris Swallowtail (*Papilio paris*) is found from China and the Himalayas south to Java (island forms probably represent a separate species). It is a fast-flying forest butterfly that is especially common near streams, where the males settle on wet sand.

◄ *Papilio ulysses*, Daintree Naional Park, Queensland, Australia

The most southeasterly of the peacock swallowtails, the Ulysses Swallowtail or Blue Mountain Butterfly (*Papilio ulysses*) is widespread in the Moluccas, New Guinea, the Solomon Islands and New Caledonia (some of the island forms may represent separate species). It is common in the rainforests of northeast Queensland, Australia, where it has become a popular tourist attraction.

▶ *Papilio machaon*, Switzerland

Papilio machaon is "the" Swallowtail, the first butterfly to carry that name. Up to 8 cm (3 in) across, it is one of the largest European butterflies. This is one of the most successful and broadly adaptable of butterflies, found from Europe to North Africa and across Asia to northern and western North America, where it is known as the Old World Swallowtail. It thrives in many different habitats, from Canadian tundra and alpine woodland to the wetlands of Norfolk, England and the coasts of the Mediterranean.

▶ Thoas, Swallowtail *(Heraclides thoas)* Rurrenabaque, Bolivia

The Thoas Swallowtail (*Heraclides thoas*), one of 143 American swallowtails, ranges from Mexico to Argentina. Its caterpillars feed on plants in the pepper family (Piperaceae). The caterpillars of its extremely similar cousin the Giant Swallowtail (*Heraclides cresphontes*), known as "orange dogs," feed instead on citrus and its relatives, and can strip the leaves from young orange trees. Nonetheless, butterfly gardeners in the United States often plant small citrus trees to attract and produce Giant Swallowtails.

▶ *Lamproptera meges*, Gunung Leuser National Park, Northern Sumatra, Indonesia

Dragontails are unusual little swallowtails of tropical and subtropical Asian rainforests. They have disproportionately large, constantly quivering tails. There are three species; the third, from Yunnan, China, was named in 2014, 183 years after the second was described. They may have been evolving on their own for 44 million years. Male dragontails frequent fast-running streams and waterfalls. Because they undulate in flight, with rapid wingbeats, on the wing they can be mistaken for dragonflies – hence their name. This is a Green Dragontail (*Lamproptera meges*).

The skippers (Hesperiidae), named for their typical "skipping" flight, are in many ways the most distinctive of butterflies. Skippers are heavy-bodied, blunt-winged and moth-like; indeed, like moths, many fly after dark or are most active at dawn or dusk. Their antennae are knobbed like those of other butterflies, but the knobs of most species taper to a distinctively projecting curved whisker.

Although most skippers are unobtrusive brown butterflies, differing from each other only in subtle ways (they can be notoriously difficult for a butterfly-watcher to identify), they are a remarkably diverse group, with some 3,500 species divided into more than 500 genera in seven subfamilies. Many tropical American skippers are almost startlingly colorful.

The caterpillars of many skippers feed on grasses and live (and sometimes pupate) in shelters that they build by folding or rolling bits of leaf and securing them with silk.

▶ *Burara gomata radiosa*, Tangkoko Nature Reserve, North Sulawesi, Indonesia

The subfamily Coeliadinae, the awls (about 150 species), may be the oldest skipper lineage. Restricted to the tropics of the Old World, awls are fast-flying insects that often land under leaves. They perch with their wings closed. The 14 species of *Burara* are large, thick-bodied skippers, generally orange or greenish brown above. They are most active in the early morning or at dusk. The Pale Green Awlet (*Burara gomata*) ranges from India to Sulawesi.

Spread-wing skippers (subfamily Pyrginae) occur worldwide but are most strongly represented in the New World tropics. Their tropical American members include some of the most colorful of all skippers. Most skippers in this subfamily perch with their wings open (hence the name "flat" applied to a number of species), though some fold them over the back; the North American cloudywings (*Thorybes*) hold them partly open. The subfamily is divided into seven tribes.

◄ *Myscelus phoronis,* **Manu National Park, Peru**
The firetips (Tribe Pyrrhopygini) range from the American Southwest to Argentina. They were formerly placed in a subfamily of their own. Uniquely among skippers, both caterpillars and pupae are covered with long hairs, and the caterpillars are often banded or spotted with bright colors. Many adult firetips have abdomens tipped with bright red – hence their English and scientific names. The Sunburst Glory (*Myscelus phoronis*) lives in humid forests in the eastern Andes at elevations between 400 and 1,800 m (1,300–5,900 ft).

▶ *Tagiades japetus,*
Crystal Cascades,
Queensland, Australia

Tagiades japetus is known as the Pied Flat in Australia and the Common Snow Flat in Asia. It is found from India to the Solomon Islands and coastal Queensland, Australia. Its tribe, the Tagiadini, ranges from Africa to Australia. Pied Flats lay their eggs on leaves of species of *Dioscorea*. The young caterpillars make tents for themselves by cutting and folding bits of leaf, moving to larger shelters as they grow and finally pupating in a shelter made by binding two leaves together with silk.

▶ *Anastrus obscurus,*
Risaralda, Colombia

Anastrus obscurus belongs to a genus of 11 species found from Mexico to Argentina. It is one of more than 100 species of tropical American skippers, from many genera, whose males (and, much more rarely, females) attend columns of army ants. Birds follow the ants to snatch up insects flushed out by the marauding ant columns, and the skippers are there to feed on the birds' droppings. From the droppings the males get sodium and nitrogen, some of which they pass on to the females during mating.

▲ *Carterocephalus palaemon*, Aargau Jura Park, Switzerland

The Chequered Skipper (*Carterocephalus palaemon*), called the Arctic Skipper in North America, is one of the skipperlings (subfamily Heteropterinae), a widely distributed group of slimly built skippers whose larvae feed on grasses and related plants. It is a northern butterfly of meadows, glades and grassy bogs in coniferous or mixed woodland. In North America it is rare south of Canada, except in the far west. In Scotland, Chequered Skippers prefer south-facing sheltered areas, where they hide deep in the grass tussocks during inclement weather.

◀ *Spialia sertorius*, Switzerland

The Red-underwing Skipper (*Spialia sertorius*) is one of a genus of largely African skippers. This is primarily a central and southern European species, and occurs elsewhere only in northwest Africa. It is a butterfly of dry grasslands, found where its larval food plants, including Salad Burnet (*Sanguisorba minor*), grow. Red-underwing Skippers overwinter as caterpillars before pupating in the leaf litter, in a cocoon of plant remains. The adults fly from May to July and, in some areas, in a second brood later in the summer.

The grass skippers (subfamily Hesperiinae) are a large group of small, mostly orange or brown butterflies. They typically rest with their wings closed or in a unique "jet plane" position, in which the hindwings are held farther open than the forewings, giving the butterfly the look of a tiny delta-wing aircraft. As their name suggests, the caterpillars of most species feed on grasses. Males of most species have a sex brand, or stigma: a patch of black androconial scales on the forewing. These scales produce pheromones that can be wafted toward a suitable female.

◄ *Thymelicus lineola*, Switzerland

The Essex Skipper (*Thymelicus lineola*) is native to temperate Eurasia and North Africa. It was accidentally introduced in Ontario, Canada, in 1910. The European Skipper (as North Americans call it) now ranges from Newfoundland to North Dakota and South Carolina, with a western population – perhaps established through eggs shipped in hay bales – from British Columbia to Colorado. It is still spreading. Its caterpillars feed on a variety of grasses and live in rolled-up tubes of grass held together with silk.

Thymelicus sylvestris, Switzerland

The Small Skipper (*Thymelicus sylvestris*) is abundant in areas of tall grass over much of Europe, North Africa and the Middle East. It is very similar to the Essex Skipper (*T. lineola*), differing in minor details such as the color of the underside of the tips of the antennae: dull reddish in *T. sylvestris*, glossy black in *T. lineola*. Adults visit the flowers of clover, thistles, dandelions and other weedy plants. They roost, sometimes by the hundreds, in sunlit patches of tall grass, often together with Essex Skippers.

Suniana sunias, Royal National Park, Australia

The Orange Dart or Wide-brand Grass-dart (*Suniana sunias*) is a butterfly of the forest edge that ranges from the Moluccas and New Guinea to northern and eastern Australia. Males are strongly territorial, guarding their territory from a blade of grass and flying in pursuit of any intruder. Orange Dart caterpillars are green, with black heads. They feed on a variety of grasses and construct tubular shelters by binding together blades of grass with silk. Within these shelters they rest and, eventually, pupate.

Hesperia comma, Alps, Switzerland

The Common Branded Skipper (*Hesperia comma*) is found throughout much of the temperate northern hemisphere. In Britain it is known as the Silver-spotted Skipper, but in North America (where most other *Hesperia* species live) that name is used for another butterfly, *Epargyreus clarus* (subfamily Eudaminae). Common Branded Skippers usually have one brood per year. In the Far North, each brood, like some other arctic butterflies, lives for two years, overwintering as eggs in their first year and as caterpillars or pupae in their second.

and gardens.

Pierids probably originated in temperate Eurasia, but today the 1,100-odd species in the family range almost throughout the world. They are missing only in New Zealand – where the Cabbage White has been introduced – the islands of the South Pacific and the Antarctic. Most live in the tropics, but some reach extremes of latitude and altitude. Hecla and Labrador Sulphurs (*Colias hecla* and *C. nastes*) penetrate the Arctic to 83°N at the northern tip of Canada's Ellesmere Island, while pierids in the Himalayas and the Andes may reach 5,000 m (16,000 ft) above sea level.

are usually larger than females.

The Pieridae is divided into four subfamilies: Pierinae (whites, marbles and orangetips), Coliadinae (sulphurs and yellows), Dismorphiinae (wood whites and mimic sulphurs) and Pseudopontiinae; the last contains five species (formerly lumped together as one) of delicate, pure white West and Central African butterflies. Pseudopontiines are unusual in lacking clubs on the antennae, a distinguishing feature of other butterflies.

◄ *Anthocharis cardamines*, Switzerland

Only the male sports the bright colors that give the Orange-tip (*Anthocharis cardamines*) its name. In Britain, where it flies as early as April, the male is a harbinger of spring, but in the high mountains of central Europe males may not appear until midsummer. Females emerge a few weeks later to lay their eggs on Cuckoo Flower (*Cardamine pratensis*), Garlic Mustard (*Alliaria petiolata*) and similar plants. Orange-tips are common in damp meadows, hedgerows and alpine grasslands from western Europe to Japan.

◄ *Pieris rapae*, Switzerland

The Cabbage White or Cabbage Butterfly (*Pieris rapae*), a native of Europe (where it is known as the Small White) and Asia, was accidentally introduced to North America in the 1860s and to Australia and New Zealand in 1929. It has become one of the commonest butterflies in all three areas. Over much of its range it is now a serious agricultural pest. Its larvae, known as cabbageworms, destroy cabbages, broccoli and similar plants, stripping the leaves and burrowing into the heads as the plants mature.

◄ *Pieris bryoniae*, Alps, Switzerland

The Mountain Green-veined White (*Pieris bryoniae*), true to its name, is a butterfly of mountain forest clearings, rocky slopes and damp alpine meadows above about 1,000 m (3,300 ft) elevation. It ranges across mountain peaks from the Juras of Switzerland and France to the Tian Shan Mountains of central Asia. Its larvae feed on alpine members of the cabbage family (Brassicaceae), particularly Buckler Mustard (*Biscutella laevigata*). A single brood – or, more rarely and at lower elevations, two broods – flies in spring and summer.

Pontia edusa, Switzerland

The Eastern Bath White (*Pontia edusa*) is an eastern European and Asian version of the better-known Bath White (*P. daplidice*) of western Europe. It is a butterfly of warm, dry, open country. Several overlapping broods fly during the course of a season, with the pupae surviving over the winter. Both Bath Whites are migrants and are occasionally found north of their normal range. The name "Bath White" dates to a needlework image of a wandering *P. daplidice* found near the city of Bath, England, in 1795.

▼ *Perrhybris lypera sulphuralis*, Alluriquin, Ecuador

Though males of the three species in the tropical American genus *Perrhybris* resemble typical whites, females such as this *P. lypera* are "tiger mimics" – members of a complex of unpalatable orange-and-black butterflies. They appear to mimic tigerwing butterflies in the longwing genus *Mechanitis*, and also imitate their manner of flight. *P. lypera* ranges from Costa Rica to Ecuador. It lives in the rainforest understory, where females lay their eggs in clusters on plants in the caper and (possibly) laurel families.

JEZEBELS

Delias

Delias contains more species than any other butterfly genus: 255 at last count. Its members, known as jezebels, have been diversifying for more than 20 million years. They probably arose in the Australasian region but repeatedly spread north into Asia. Today they range from Australia, New Guinea (where the greatest number of species live) and the southwest Pacific to the Himalayas, India and China. Jezebel larvae feed mostly on – and take up toxins from – a range of mistletoes; as their bright colors warn us, the adult butterflies are unpalatable. Many species mimic one another and are imitated in turn by other butterflies and day-flying moths.

Delias hyparete, Chiang Mai, Thailand

The Painted Jezebel (*Delias hyparete*) ranges from India to the
Philippines. Once confined to rainforests, it is now widespread and
common in many types of habitats, including urban gardens. For
much of the day it flutters through the treetops, but it comes to rest
in the forest understory late in the day. Its main larval food plant is
the parasitic mistletoe *Dendrophthoe pentandra*. Jezebel caterpillars
live in groups and devour mistletoe leaves with such thoroughness
that the plant frequently dies.

Delias nigrina, Bunya Mountains, Australia

The Black, or Common, Jezebel
(*Delias nigrina*) is a well-known
butterfly of eastern Australia,
east of the Great Dividing
Range, where it frequents vine
thickets and rainforests as

▲ *Mylothris croceus*, Bwindi Impenetrable National Park, Uganda
The caterpillars of the African dotted borders (51 species of *Mylothris*) feed on toxic plants, especially mistletoes (Loranthaceae), and adults are known to be distasteful to birds. They advertise their unpalatability with bright colors and slow, deliberate flight, and a number of other butterflies mimic them. The Orange Dotted Border (*Mylothris croceus*) is a highland forest butterfly from Rwanda, Uganda and the eastern Democratic Republic of Congo. The Bwindi Forest, where this one was photographed, is home to more than 200 species of butterflies.

▶ *Aporia crataegi*, Switzerland
The Black-veined White (*Aporia crataegi*) vanished from Britain in 1925. It is still common across Europe, North Africa and temperate Asia, though populations can fluctuate wildly. Black-veined Whites roost communally, with several butterflies clinging to a single flower head. Females have a peculiar (and so far unexplained) habit, not shared by males, of rubbing their wings together until the scales fall off. The caterpillars feed on the leaves of hawthorns (*Crataegus* spp.) and related fruit trees such as apple, cherry, peach and plum.

◄ *Gonepteryx rhamni*, Switzerland

Brimstone is an old word for sulfur, so the butter-yellow wings of the Brimstone (*Gonepteryx rhamni*) give it its common name. Adults emerge in late spring or summer. They hibernate in dense evergreen bushes from September until they emerge in the following spring to breed and die. Though the Brimstone is common and widespread in Europe, North Africa and temperate Asia, it's distribution is limited by the availability of its larval food plants, members of the buckthorn family (Rhamnaceae – hence the Latin species name *rhamni*).

◄ *Colias alfacariensis*, Switzerland
▼ *Colias hyale*, Switzerland

The butterflies of the genus *Colias*, called clouded yellows in Europe and (with others in the Coliadinae) sulphurs in North America, form a large group with complex evolutionary interrelationships, confused in many cases by hybridization. Clouded yellows are found across the northern hemisphere and in South America and Africa. Some migrate in enormous numbers. A swarm of more than 100,000 Clouded Yellows (*Colias crocea*) was recorded crossing the English Channel in 1947.

The Pale Clouded Yellow (*Colias hyale*) and the closely related Berger's Clouded Yellow (*Colias alfacariensis*) were not recognized as separate species until 1945. They remain extremely difficult to tell apart as adults, but their caterpillars are distinctive. Both species range widely across Europe and temperate Asia.

▲ *Colias palaeno* male, Switzerland
▶ *Colias palaeno* female, Switzerland

Colias palaeno is a bog-haunting butterfly with a huge range, from western Europe across temperate Asia and northern North America. It is known as the Moorland Clouded Yellow in Britain (where it is a rare straggler) and the Palaeno Sulphur in North America. These individuals are feeding at Bellflowers (*Campanula cochleariifolia*). The fringe of reddish hairs along their wing margins will likely wear off as they age. In the video game *Ace Attorney*, the character "Colias Palaeno" is an ambassador from a fictional country.

◀▲ *Phoebis sennae*, Colombia (captive)
The Cloudless, or Cloudless Giant, Sulphur (*Phoebis sennae*) is common from the southern United States through the West Indies, Central America and South America to southernmost Argentina. It gets its name from the clear (cloudless) lemon yellow of the upper surface of its wings. The Cloudless Sulphur is a well-known migrant in North America, heading south to Florida in the autumn in numbers that may rival migrating swarms of Monarchs (*Danaus plexippus*). Wanderers may stray northward and on occasion even reach southeastern Ontario, Canada.

◀ *Eurema hecabe*, Gunung Leuser National Park, Sumatra, Indonesia
More than 70 species of grass yellows (*Eurema* spp.) flutter low over disturbed grassy areas in the warmer parts of world. The Large or Common Grass Yellow (*Eurema hecabe*) is a variable and highly migratory butterfly with a wide range of host plants; it is found almost anywhere throughout Africa, tropical Asia, much of Australia and the South Pacific. It can occur in huge swarms and may be the most abundant butterfly in the world. Broods emerging in summer are darker, a change apparently triggered by increasing day length.

Leptidea sinapis, Switzerland

The eight wood whites (*Leptidea*) are the only Eurasian members of the subfamily Dismorphiinae, whose members otherwise live almost entirely in the American tropics. Their slow, delicate flight is very different from the rapid flight of most other pierids. The Wood White (*Leptidea sinapis*) is found across Europe and northern Asia. Genetic studies have shown that European *L. sinapis* are really a complex of three almost identical species. The most recently discovered, the Cryptic Wood White (*L. juvernica*) of Ireland, was detected only in 2011.

Dismorphia medora, Manu National Park, Peru

The Medora Mimic White (*Dismorphia medora*) of the northern Andes is one of more than 50 dismorphiine butterflies in tropical America. Many are members of long-winged black and orange "tiger mimic" complexes that include other pierids and butterflies from other families. Multiple mimicry complexes can coexist in one place. One mimetic butterfly and moth community, at Rancho Grande, Venezuela, involved at least 48 different species, including Medora Mimic Whites. His studies of *Dismorphia*, a genus of 30 species, inspired Henry Walter Bates to write his classic paper on mimicry in 1861.

The enormous family Nymphalidae encompasses a huge range of the world's butterflies: some 6,000 species in 550 genera. Nymphalids range from the giant, glittering morphos of the New World tropics to tiny checkerspots no bigger than a fingernail. They are united by, among other things, a shared pattern of three parallel ridges – found in no other Lepidoptera – on the undersides of their antennae and, most noticeably, conversion of their front limbs into clawless shortened stumps that are useless, in most nymphalids, for walking or perching. In males these limbs are covered with hair-like scales; it is to them that nymphalids owe their common name "brush-footed butterflies."

Currently the family is divided into 12 subfamilies, a number of which were once considered families in their own right. This section includes nine of them, omitting only the most ancient: the Libytheinae (snouts or beaks); the Calinaginae, comprising the enigmatic Asian genus *Calinaga*, which includes the oddly named Freak (*C. buddha*); and the Pseudergolinae, members of four Asian genera, including the Tabby (*Pseudergolis wedah*). Among the subfamilies included here, the Charaxinae and Satyrinae, Heliconiinae and Limenitidinae, Biblidinae and Apaturinae, and Cyrestinae and Nymphalinae are believed to be, respectively, each others' closest relatives.

▶ *Cithaerias pireta, Braulio Carillo National Park, Costa Rica*
The wings of the Pink-tipped Glasswing Satyr (Cithaerias pireta, Subfamily Satyrinae) of central and northwestern South America have lost almost all of their scales, but retain the bars and eyespots of the ancestral nymphalid ground plan (see p. 16). Scales still form the eyespots, but the wing bars of Cithaerias, uniquely in the family, are marked directly on the wing membrane itself.

The milkweed butterflies (Danaiinae) include among their number one of the most famous and iconic of insects, the Monarch butterfly (*Danaus plexippus*). Typical danaiines (Tribe Danaiini) lay their eggs on various species of milkweed (*Asclepias*). From them their caterpillars absorb cardiac glycosides, toxins that can induce vomiting and even heart failure in birds and other vertebrates. They take up other toxins from nectars they feed on as adults, so both caterpillars and adults carry bright or contrasting warning colors and patterns. This makes the Danaiini ideal models for a host of mimics from other butterfly and moth lineages. Even more involved in mimicry is the related tribe Ithomiini (clearwings and tiger mimics), a tropical American radiation of some 370 unpalatable species. Most take up toxic alkaloids as adults, from the nectars of members of the daisy and borage families (Asteraceae and Boraginaceae). The Ithomiini provided model examples for the original 19th-century descriptions of both Batesian and Müllerian mimicry.

◄ *Danaus chrysippus*, Jozani Chwaka Bay National Park, Zanzibar, Tanzania
Outside of the Americas the Monarch is replaced by a number of similarly distasteful butterflies (and their mimics, including whites, swallowtails and moths). The African Monarch, or Plain Tiger (*Danaus chrysippus*) is common in many habitats from semi-desert to gardens, farms and open woodland. It ranges throughout Africa and from the coasts of the Mediterranean eastward through India and Southeast Asia to Australia.

◄ *Parantica melaneus*, Saiyok National Park, Thailand
The Chocolate Tiger (*Parantica melaneus*), found from India and China to the Malay Peninsula, is one of a number of similar Asian and tropical Australasian species that are mostly black or dark brown and white, often with a blue sheen or a yellowish tinge. It is common in and around forested areas, where it is often seen feeding at roadside and garden flowers. Like many distasteful butterflies, *Parantica* tigers fly slowly. Their flight is imitated by mimics, including female wanderers (*Pareronia* spp.).

◀ *Idea stolli*, Tanjung Puting National Park, Kalimantan, Indonesia

The graceful, slow flight of the Common Tree Nymph (*Idea stolli*), like a floating scrap of paper, gives it its Malay name, *surat* ("letter"). One of 12 *Idea* species in tropical Asia, it seems delicate despite its size (females are up to 18 cm/7 in across). Widespread in forests from the Malay Peninsula to Borneo, Sumatra and Java, Common Tree Nymphs glide through the treetops feeding (sometimes in large numbers) at flowering trees before spiraling down to rest in the shade on a low bush.

▶ *Tellervo zoilus*, The Boulders, Babinda, Queensland, Australia

The nine species of *Tellervo* are black-and-white rainforest butterflies with striking yellow or orange eyes, found in New Guinea, the Solomon Islands and tropical Queensland, Australia. Thought to be closest to the New World Ithomiini, they are usually placed in their own tribe, Tellervini. Bad-tasting like other danaiines, they are models for a number of mimics. The Hamadryad (*Tellervo zoilus*) is common in north-east Queensland, where it flies slowly through the understory. Males gather in sunny patches to advertise for females in communal display grounds, or leks.

▶ *Heterosais nephele nephele*, Tambopata National Reserve, Peru

The Ithomiini are delicate, long-winged butter-flies that fly, mostly in the depths of the forest understory, from Mexico to Argentina. Most, if not all, are involved in extensive Müllerian mimicry complexes, particularly the orange-and-black "tiger mimic" complexes that include other ithomiines, other butterflies, moths and even a damselfly. Clearwing butterflies like this *Heterosais nephele* have lost many of the scales that make most butterfly wings opaque, and have reduced others to tiny hairs. Their wings are thus largely transparent, except along the veins and wing margins.

The 395 species of leafwings (Charaxinae) are mostly tropical forest butterflies, though a few species extend to temperate areas, including the Mediterranean and southern Australia. The large Old World genus *Charaxes* (the gladiators), highly prized by collectors, is most numerous in Africa, where there are 179 species. Many leafwings have ornate color patterns and distinctive irregular shapes, and most have one or more pairs of short tails on the hindwing. Strong, agile flyers with powerful flight muscles, they spend much of their time in the canopy or basking in sunlit patches on the forest floor. They feed on rotting fruit, tree sap, carrion or dung.

Fountainea nessus,
**Manu National Park,
Peru**

This is a male Superb Leafwing
(*Fountainea nessus*), one of the
many South American charax-
ines and one of eight species
in the genus *Fountainea*. It is
found at middle elevations
in the eastern Andes from
Venezuela to northeastern
Argentina. Like many leafwings,
its bright colors are confined to
its upper side. With its wings
closed it resembles a dead leaf
and can be difficult to detect on
the forest floor, where it feeds
on rotting fruit and carrion.

The 2,400 or so species in the nine recognized tribes of browns (subfamily Satyrinae) were once divided among four separate subfamilies. They include butterflies as seemingly different as the huge morphos and owls of tropical American forests and the hardy, subtly patterned graylings of alpine screes. Though some are brilliantly colorful and iridescent, most satyrines are, as their name implies, largely brown. Rounded eyespots mark the wings of many species, particularly on the underside.

Satyrines may have evolved as feeders on palm leaves, and the caterpillars of tropical butterflies such as the Palm King (Amathusia phidippus) of Southeast Asia still feed on palms today. However, at some point what became the major lineage in the subfamily switched from palms to grasses and sedges. That change led to the evolution of many more species in the tropics and allowed the browns to follow their new food plants well into the colder reaches of the temperate zone.

Palm Kings and Others

Tribe Amathusiini

Members of the tropical Asian and Australasian tribe Amathusiini are mostly large, broad-winged butterflies of the forest floor. They keep close to the ground, fly mostly at dusk or after dark, and can be very difficult to detect as they rest in the leaf litter. Amathusiines feed on fallen fruits and tree sap and do not visit flowers.

▶ *Faunis canens,* Kheaun Sri Nakarin National Park, Thailand

The Common Faun (*Faunis canens*) of India and Southeast Asia is the best-known of the 14 species in its genus. One of the smaller and less colorful amathusiines, it has a wingspan of 5.5 to 6.5 cm (2–2.6 in). Its bright reddish brown upperwings are usually visible only if the butterfly is startled into flight. Common Fauns feed on fallen fruit, often with other butterflies, and lay their eggs on wild bananas (*Musa* spp.).

▲ *Taenaris catops*, Lae, Papua New Guinea

The Silky Owl (*Taenaris catops*) of New Guinea is a large, variable and spectacular butterfly. Up to 9.5 cm (3.7 in) across, it has strongly rounded hindwings and impressive eyespots. It keeps to the forest understory but, unlike most amathusiines, is active by day. Silky Owl caterpillars feed in large groups on wild bananas, betel palms (*Areca* spp.) and cabbage trees (*Cordyline* spp.), among others. Adults are attracted to cycads and feed on their juices. Cycad juices are rich in toxins, and the adults' coloring may be a warning to predators.

◄ *Caligo eurilochus*,
Tambopata National
Reserve, Peru

Tropical American owls (Tribe
Brassolini) live in the depths of
the forest and seldom fly except
just before dusk and at night.
The Forest Giant Owl (*Caligo
eurilochus*), found in forest
depths from southern Mexico
to the Amazon Basin, is one of
the largest, with a wingspan
of up to 13.5 cm (5.3 in). It is
iridescent grayish blue bordered with blackish on its upper
side, but it is the underside,
with its impressive eyespots,
that we usually see as it perches
on a tree trunk or feeds on rotting fruit on the forest floor.

◄ *Cithaerias pireta*, Braulio Carillo National Park, Costa Rica
▲ *Cithaerias aurorina*, Amacayacu National Park, Colombia

Blushing Phantoms or Glasswing Satyrs (*Cithaerias pireta* and *C. aurorina*) belong
to the small, dusk-haunting tropical American tribe Haeterini. They are attracted
to rotting fruit and fly just above the ground in the deep shade of the humid forest
floor, usually around sunlit gaps where males apparently defend territories. Most
have largely transparent wings with lustrous patches of rose, purple or blue.
They can be difficult to see once they settle. Haeterines lay their eggs on arums
(Araceae), which are among the few toxic host plants used by satyrine butterflies.
The Pink-tipped Glasswing Satyr (*C. pireta*) lays on *Philodendron herbaceum*, a
common understory vine.

Browns

Tribe Satyrini

Satyrini, the typical browns, form by far the largest tribe in the Satyrinae – a quarter of all the species in the entire family Nymphalidae belong within it. Its members, grouped into 13 or 14 separate subtribes, occur almost throughout the world. Most members of this group lay their eggs on grasses or sedges, and many have colonized the arctic tundra or high alpine meadows.

◄ *Chloreuptychia arnaca*, Corcovado National Park, Costa Rica
The Blue-smudged Satyr (*Chloreuptychia arnaca*) is found throughout most of the American tropics. It spends the day sitting quietly in the rainforest undergrowth, flying only short distances in sunlit forest openings. It feeds on bird droppings, rotting fruit and decomposing fungi. Females lay their eggs in the late afternoon on clumps of forest grasses. Their caterpillars have stout, spiny head horns, and their pupae, instead of hanging downward, stick out horizontally from the stems to which they have attached.

◄ *Mycalesis patiana*, Kinabatangan River, Sabah, Malaysia
The 230-odd bushbrowns (Subtribe Mycalesina), common butterflies found from Africa to northeastern Australia, represent what has been called one of the more spectacular evolutionary radiations of butterflies in the Old World tropics. Bushbrown larvae feed on grasses, sedges, gingers, palms and related plants. Adults prefer rotten fruit but may visit flowers. The Malayan Bushbrown (*Mycalesis patiana*), one of 88 species in *Mycalesis*, ranges from India to Borneo. Common along forest trails, it flies quickly and usually close to the ground, with frequent stops.

Coenonympha pamphilus, Switzerland

Most of the butterflies in the subtribe Coenonymphina are Australasian, but the 42 species of *Coenonympha* range across Eurasia, North Africa and North America. The Small Heath (*Coenonympha pamphilus*), one of the most widespread, is found over a broad range of mostly open habitats from Europe and northwest Africa east to Mongolia. Males patrol their territories or perch, often on sun-warmed stones, waiting for virgin females (mated females tend to avoid male territories). Their caterpillars feed on a variety of grasses.

Cepheuptychia cephus, Amacayacu National Park, Colombia

The Cephus Satyr (*Cepheuptychia cephus*) lives in tropical South America, including Trinidad. It belongs to the subtribe Euptychiina, a radiation of some 400 species of little-known tropical American butterflies, plus a single species confined to Taiwan. Euptychiines live low in the forest understory, shunning bright light. Some fly mostly at dawn or dusk. The upperwings of the Cephus Satyr are largely iridescent blue. They probably reflect strongly in the ultraviolet, an adaptation to help the sexes find one another in the forest depths.

◄ *Oressinoma typhla*, El Avila National Park, Venezuela

The two species of *Oressinoma*, also members of the Coenonymphina, are small butterflies that live in the American tropics. The Common Oressinoma or Typhla Satyr (*Oressinoma typhla*) lives in wet areas of rainforest and cloud forest on mountain slopes from Costa Rica to Bolivia. Adults feed on rotting fruit, decomposing fungi and occasionally dung. Their caterpillars feed at night on forest sedges. A courting male flies above a female, lands beside her and then touches her antennae with his own as he vibrates his wings.

◄ *Aphantopus hyperantus*, Switzerland

The Ringlet (*Aphantopus hyperantus*) belongs to the small subtribe Maniolina, a largely European group with a few North African and Asian species and a single isolated member, the Red-bordered Satyr (*Gyrocheilus patrobas*), in Arizona and northern Mexico. The Ringlet is common across much of Europe and temperate Asia. It prefers open woodlands, hedgerows and other areas where the grasses are lush and it can avoid the sun.

◄ *Melanargia galathea*, Switzerland

Melanargia, with 20 Eurasian species, is the only genus In the subtribe Melanargiina. Unlike most satyrines, melanargiines are toxic to predators. Though the caterpillars feed on nontoxic grasses, they may take up alkaloids from a fungus that parasitizes the plants. Adults look and fly more like unpalatable whites (Pieridae) than other browns. The Marbled White (*Melanargia galathea*) lives on dry grasslands and rocky slopes in Europe and North Africa. It can be abundant but may disappear when meadows are replaced by trees or farmland.

GRAYLINGS

Oenis and *Hipparchia*

These three Swiss butterflies are members of the largest Satyrine sub-tribe, the Satyrina. All three are single-brooded, overwinter as caterpillars and pupate on or near the ground.

◄ *Hipparchia genava,* Switzerland
The Lesser Woodland Grayling (*Hipparchia genava*) is a localized montane endemic found only in the mountains of southern France, Switzerland and Italy. It is almost indistinguishable from the more widespread Woodland Grayling (*H. alcyone*)

◄ *Oeneis glacialis,* Alps, Switzerland
The Alpine Grayling (*Oeneis glacialis*) is another localized endemic, confined to dry montane grasslands and rocky slopes between 1,400 and 2,900 m (4,600–9,500 ft) and most frequently over 1,700 m (5,600 ft) in the European Alps. It is one of the arctics (*Oeneis*), a genus widely distributed in boreal and mountain regions of North America and Eurasia, with some species ranging across both landmasses.

▶ *Chazara briseis,* Switzerland
The Hermit (*Chazara briseis*) is a butterfly of hot, dry grasslands in southern Europe and North Africa. It rests on shady tree trunks during the hottest part of the day. It is listed as Near Threatened by IUCN and has been considered endangered in central Europe.

RINGLETS

Erebia

All but one of the roughly 100 species of mostly alpine and arctic butterflies in the subtribe Erebiina belong to the genus *Erebia*. Its members are scattered across temperate Eurasia to North America. Some occur on both continents, but many local *Erebia* species apparently evolved on mountain ranges isolated during the Pleistocene epoch

◄ *Erebia pandrose*, Alps, Switzerland
The Dewy Ringlet (*Erebia pandrose*) is found in mountain ranges and arctic tundra across Europe and Asia. In the Pyrenees, the southeastern Alps and the Durmitor and Altai ranges in Montenegro and Kazakhstan, it is replaced by the similar False Dewy Ringlet (*E. sthennyo*). The two interbreed along a narrow belt in the Alps. In the past they apparently spread from one range to another during different interglacial epochs, so they rarely met on the open plains and thus could not interbreed.

◄ *Erebia ligea*, Alps, Switzerland
Erebia species can be difficult to identify, but the Arran Brown (*Erebia ligea*) can be distinguished at close range by the interrupted checkerboard-like fringe along the borders of its wings. There are two separate populations, one in Finland and Scandinavia, where it can be found even along the seashore, and the other centered on the mountains of central Europe. The Arran Brown gets its English name from a stray individual captured on the Isle of Arran, Scotland, in 1803.

▶ *Erebia alberganus*, Switzerland
Large numbers of Almond-eyed Ringlets (*Erebia alberganus*) may concentrate in flower-rich mountain forest glades from mid-June to early August. There are three isolated populations in the Alps, the Apennines of Italy, and the Stara and Korab Mountains in Bulgaria and Macedonia.

▼ *Erebia pharte*, Alps, Switzerland
The Blind Ringlet (*Erebia pharte*) can see as well as any butterfly. It gets its name because the orange eyespots on its wings lack dark "pupils." Blind Ringlets fly in high grassy meadows around the treeline in the Alps, Tatras and Carpathians, especially in areas with tall grass and at the edges of woodlands. Its caterpillars feed on a variety of grasses and sedges, depending on habitat; they hibernate twice and pupate, suspended between spun-together grass stalks, at the end of May.

The subfamily Heliconiinae includes some of the most popular, beautiful and heavily studied of tropical butterflies. Many of the most frequently encountered inmates of butterfly houses worldwide are heliconiines, and so are the fritillaries of the temperate northern hemisphere. Many tropical species are unpalatable and form parts of extensive mimicry rings, particularly in Africa and South America. The Heliconiinae is divided into four tribes, two – Acraeini and Heliconiini – once considered families on their own. The genus *Cethosia*, the Asian and Australasian lacewing butterflies, does not fit neatly into this classification; it may deserve a tribe of its own, though it is closest to the Acraeini.

Acraeas

Tribe Acraeini

Acraea and *Actinote*, the two genera in the Acraeini, are long-winged, colorful, unpalatable butterflies found in the Old and New Worlds respectively. The tribe is particularly diverse in Africa; only six of the roughly 200 species in *Acraea*, and less than half of the 145 species in *Actinote*, are found elsewhere. Many species in both genera are models for Batesian mimicry by other butterflies.

◄ **Cethosia hypsea, Malaysia (captive)**
The broad, scalloped wings of the 15 to 17 species of lacewings (*Cethosia*) are mostly red, black and white above and intricately decorated below with patterns of black, white, red, orange and yellow. Lacewings range from India through Southeast Asia to New Guinea, the Solomon Islands and tropical Australia. The Malayan Lacewing (*C. hypsea*) is found from southern Myanmar (Burma) through the Malay Peninsula to Java, Borneo and the Philippines. It is often seen visiting flowers along the forest edge or fluttering among the bushes along a wooded trail.

Passion-vine Butterflies

Tribe Heliconiini

The graceful and seemingly delicate passion-vine butterflies, which are widespread in the warmer parts of the Americas, make up the tribe Heliconiini. Linnaeus, the father of systematic zoology, thought they were too feminine-looking to be named for a Greek hero such as Danaus (his name would do for the Monarch) and instead named the genus *Heliconius*, after Mount Helicon, home of the Muses. Entomologists have since followed suit, naming individual species after the Muses, the Graces, classical heroines such as Dido, the tragic queen of Carthage, and, more recently, artists and poets. One genus, *Neruda*, is named for the Chilean poet and politician Pablo Neruda (1904–73).

◀ *Philaethria dido*, Rurrenabaque, Bolivia
The Dido Longwing or Scarce Bamboo Page (*Philaethria dido*) is the most widespread of nine extremely similar species, some quite rare and local, ranging from Mexico to Bolivia and Brazil. They resemble the more common Malachite (*Siproeta stelenes*), though all the butterflies involved appear to be palatable. *Philaethria* caterpillars feed on older passionflower leaves, where they mimic bird droppings. Adults fly rapidly through the rainforest canopy, ignoring flowers, but – unlike other heliconi-ines – sometimes descend to the forest floor to feed on fresh mammal dung.

◀ *Dryadula phaetusa*, Colombia (captive)
The Orange-banded Longwing or Orange Tiger (*Dryadula phaetusa*), the only member of its genus, is common along riverbanks and road-sides and in pastures from Mexico to Brazil and Argentina. It is marked on its upper side with bands of black and bright orange. Males patrol for females in the early afternoon. Several may pursue a female, flapping their wings rapidly to fan pheromones in her direction, then alight beside her and tap her with their antennae. These butterflies are roosting, hanging suspended from a stem.

▶ *Dryas iulia*, Risaralda, Colombia

The Julia Heliconian or Flambeau (*Dryas iulia*), also the only member of its genus, is common from Florida and south Texas to Brazil and throughout the West Indies. It has strayed as far north as Nebraska. Julias are "trapline" foragers, flying from flower cluster to flower cluster along a set route. Males spend much of the day searching for females. They often seek mineral salts on the ground and will feed on the eye secretions of caimans and South American river turtles.

The butterflies of the genus *Heliconius*, with their (usually) basic black marked with streaks or blotches of red, orange, white or yellow, are not only beautiful – they are highly popular attractions in butterfly gardens – but have also been of great scientific importance. They appear to have diversified extremely rapidly, resulting today in a dazzling assortment of highly varied and colorfully patterned species, 43 in all, many of them mimics of one another. Subspecies of the same group may look more like other species sharing their habitat than like their own nearest relatives, a phenomenon that has fascinated scientists for almost two centuries. Probably no other insects – the fruit fly (*Drosophila melanogaster*) aside – have been the subject of so many studies into their genetics and evolution.

◄ *Heliconius clysonymus*, Farallones de Cali, Colombia

The red bands on the wings of the Montane, Yellow or Clysonymus Longwing (*Heliconius clysonymus*) are present in some subspecies but absent in others. This is a cloud-forest butterfly found from sea level to 2,500 m (8,200 ft) in the mountains from Costa Rica to Peru. It is commonest at elevations between about 800 and 2,000 m (2,600–6,600 ft), above the lowland range of its close relative the extremely variable and much studied Common Longwing or Red Postman (*H. erato*).

◄ *Heliconius sara*, Alluriquin, Ecuador

The Sara Longwing (*Heliconius sara*), found from southern Mexico to southern Brazil, adds an iridescent blue blush to the usual *Heliconius* palette. Males either mate with females fresh out of the chrysalis or court them from mating territories. Territorial males tend to be slightly smaller than the males that visit chrysalises. Larger males may be better at jostling for position as the female emerges, while smaller males, which are less likely to injure their wings in a contest, seem better at expelling rivals from their territories.

▶ *Heliconius cydno cydnides*, Colombia (captive)

The White-barred, Cydno or Blue-and-white Longwing (*Heliconius cydno*) ranges from Mexico to Venezuela and Ecuador. The 13 different subspecies vary in the extent and completeness of the white bar across the wings; the differences may relate to their roles as members of different Müllerian mimicry rings. The form in Panama, for example, mimics another distasteful *Heliconius* species, *H. sapho*.

▲ *Heliconius numata bicoloratus*, Tingo Maria, Peru
Heliconius numata is an extremely variable Amazonian butterfly found from Venezuela and Peru to southern Brazil. Seven different color forms, each mimicking a different clearwing butterfly (*Melinaea* spp.), can exist together at the same site. Some carry a variant of the orange, black and yellow patterning of the widespread "tiger mimic" complex. The Peruvian race *bicoloratus* is more distinctive, but it too mimics a clearwing (*Melinaea marsaeus mothone*). This sort of mimicry is apparently controlled by a complex of genes acting as a single "supergene."

➤ *Heliconius charithonia*, Alluriquin, Ecuador
Except in south Texas, where the Red Postman (*H. erato*) flies in summer, the Zebra Longwing (*Heliconius charithonia*) – named for the three Graces or, in Greek, Charites – is the only *Heliconius* in the United States. It is common in southern Florida and south Texas and occasionally reaches New Mexico, Nebraska and South Carolina. It is widespread in the West Indies and ranges south to subtropical South America. The Zebra Longwing is a butterfly of scrub and forest edges from sea level to 1,800 m (5,000 ft).

◀ *Vindula erota*, Kheaun Sri Nakarin
National Park, Thailand

This is a male Common Cruiser (*Vindula erota*), a
well-known forest butterfly in Thailand and the
highlands of Peninsular Malaysia. The smaller and
darker Malay Cruiser (*V. dejone*) replaces it from
the Malaysian lowlands to New Guinea. Females
are darker and browner, with a broad white band
across both wings. Male cruisers often land on
the ground, seeking carrion or urine-soaked soil,
and may alight on boots or clothing in search of
mineral salts. Cruiser caterpillars feed on passion-
flowers (*Passiflora* spp.).

▶ *Terinos terpander teos*, Gunung
Leuser National Park, Sumatra,
Indonesia

The eight Assyrians (*Terinos* spp.) are Southeast
Asian and Australasian butterflies of the rainforest understory. Adults are active early in the day
but in the later hours sit quietly on the undersides
of leaves. The Royal Assyrian (*Terinos terpander*)
is found at lowland forest edges from Myanmar
to Java. In Singapore its only larval host plant
is *Rinorea anguifera*, a tree in the violet family
(Violaceae). The attractive and unusual pupa is
bright green, ornamented with a series of red and
yellow horns.

The more than 100 species of fritillaries (Tribe Argynnini) are largely butterflies of the north temperate zone, ranging into the arctic and alpine regions of both Eurasia and North America. One genus, *Yramia*, is native to temperate South America. *Euptoieta* is tropical American, with one species, the Variegated Fritillary (*E. claudia*), ranging north through much of the United States. Almost all fritillaries are orange-brown, banded and flecked with black on the upper surface and, in many species, marked below with silvery blotches, particularly on the undersurface of the hindwings.

▶ *Boloria titania*, Alps, Switzerland

Many of the small butterflies in the large genus *Boloria* live in the Far North or isolated in mountain ranges around the northern hemisphere. The Titania's or Purple Bog Fritillary (*Boloria titania*), one of the larger species at 3.5 to 4.5 cm (1.4–1.8 in) across, lives in damp broadleaf forests in southern Finland (where it is very rare) and the Baltic states, as well as in the Scottish Highlands, the Alps, the Pyrenees and the central Apennines. In Finland it overwinters as a small caterpillar, emerging to eat only with the coming of spring.

▶ *Issoria lathonia*, Switzerland

Issoria lathonia has been called the Queen of Spain Fritillary since at least 1775, when its name appeared (without explanation) in *The English Lepidoptera; or, the Aurelian's Pocket Companion*, by pioneering entomologist Moses Harris. Rare in Britain, it is fairly common in much of temperate Eurasia. Its caterpillars feed on the leaves of several violets; they even thrive on the Zinc Violet (*Viola calaminaria*), a plant that absorbs very high levels of zinc – they excrete the extra zinc in metal-laden feces.

The Admiral subfamily (Limenitidinae) was once used as a catchall grouping for brush-footed butterflies of uncertain relationships, but molecular studies have reduced it to a comparatively small group of genuinely close relatives. The subfamily is now divided into four tribes, plus a few unassigned outliers.

◄ *Lebadea martha*, **Kheaun Sri Nakarin National Park, Thailand**
The Knight (*Lebadea martha*), one of five tropical Asian and Australasian species in the tribe Parthenini, is a lowland forest butterfly found from India to Java, Borneo and Palawan. This is a male. Females are duller, with added white markings and more rounded forewings. Caterpillars feed on *Ixora* species, working back from the leaf tips in thin strips. Young (first-instar) caterpillars become encrusted with droppings, while later instars are increasingly decorated with branched spines. Adults are common in clearings, where they bask on mid-level foliage.

◄ *Adelpha lycorias lara*, **Manu National Park, Peru**
Adelpha is Greek for "sister," the English name given to the 90-odd butterflies in this large New World genus. Though they may have originated in North America, sisters are particularly diverse at low to middle elevations in the Andes, especially around 700 to 800 m (2,300–2,600 ft). The Pink-banded Sister (*Adelpha lycorias*) ranges from Venezuela to western Ecuador, Paraguay, northern Argentina and southeastern Brazil. Males are common along forest edges, where they feed on dung or carrion, but females are rarely seen.

▲ *Limenitis populi*, Switzerland
Most of the roughly 21 species of *Limenitis* live in Eurasia, but four – sometimes placed

Tropical Brushfoots

Most of the members of the subfamily Biblidinae live in the New World tropics, but a few, such as the castors (*Ariadne* spp.), are found in Africa and tropical Asia. There are six recognized tribes in the subfamily. Most biblidine caterpillars feed on members of the spurge family (Euphorbiaceae), but the larvae of two closely related tribes, Epiphilini and Callicorini – including the eighty-eights (*Diaethra* spp.) – have switched hosts, mostly to members of the soapberry family (Sapindaceae). Both plant families contain toxins that may pass to the caterpillars.

◀ *Catonephele acontius* male, Colombia (captive)
◤ *Catonephele acontius* female, Colombia (captive)
Males and females of the Acontius Firewing (*Catonephele acontius*) of the tribe Epicaliini, a wet-forest butterfly found from Colombia to Bolivia, differ so much that they were once described as separate species. Males have a tuft of long androconial scales on the underside of the forewing. They perch on tree trunks or in sunlit spots on leaves or fallen branches. Both sexes feed on rotting fruit. The mature caterpillar is bright green and studded with branched red-and-black stinging spines that may defend it against predatory ants.

▶ *Biblis hyperia*, Colombia (captive)

The Red Rim (*Biblis hyperia*) belongs to the Biblidini, a tribe that includes both Old and New World genera. The sole member of its genus, it is widespread in semi-open and dry forests from southern Texas to Paraguay. Its larval food plant, the Fireman or Noseburn (*Tragia volubilis*), is armed with stinging hairs, and the adult butterfly may be unpalatable, thanks to its toxins. Its strongly patterned wings and slow flight suggest that the Red Rim has little to fear from predators. The sexes look alike.

▶ *Batesia hypochlora*, Manu National Park, Peru

The Painted Beauty (*Batesia hypochlora*), an inhabitant of rainforests in the upper Amazon Basin, belongs to the tribe Ageroniini. Adults keep largely to the middle and lower levels of the forest, where they feed on rotting fruit, at wounds in tree trunks and, more rarely, on fresh dung or rotting mammal carcasses. They perch head-down on tree trunks or glide in slow circles in sunlit forest gaps, and are probably unpalatable. Their caterpillars feed in groups on a large forest tree, *Caryodendron orinocensis* (Euphorbiaceae family).

▲ *Diaethria marchalii*, Risaralda, Colombia

The Callicorini is a tribe of small, colorful tropical American butterflies, often with strikingly marked underwings. The Widespread Eighty-eight (*Diaethria marchalii*) is a humid-forest species found from Nicaragua to Ecuador. Like other *Diaethria* species, it looks as if it has been numbered with an 88, 89 or sometimes 80. It has a partiality for urine-soaked soil and may gather in numbers around human habitations. Mature caterpillars develop a pair of long, spiked horns, or scoli; when disturbed, they rear up and wriggle vigorously.

Hamadryas amphinome, Tambopata National Reserve, Peru

The 20 species of crackers (*Hamadryas* spp.) get their name because territorial males make a snapping sound as they chase a rival male or a female in flight, an ability lost in some species. Crackers rest head-down on tree trunks, where they blend in with the surrounding bark. They feed largely on rotting fruit. The Red Cracker (*Hamadryas amphinome*), named for the red at the base of its underwings, lives in dry secondary or disturbed forest habitats from Mexico to the Amazon Basin, including Trinidad.

Asterope leprieuri, male, Manu National Park, Peru

The tribe Epiphilini contains eight genera of fast-flying tropical American butterflies. *Asterope* butterflies are brilliantly metallic both above and below, with patches of red at the base of the underwings. Males such as this Leprieur's Glory (*Asterope eprieuri*) visit patches of soil along roadsides or on riverbanks, taking up minerals with their distinctively white proboscis. They fly up to the surrounding trees if disturbed; their flashing colors may distract predators seeking to capture them in flight.

Pyrrhogyra amphiro juani, Risaralda, Colombia

The Amphiro Redring (*Pyrrhogyra amphiro*) of tropical South America is one of a genus of six strikingly marked butterflies. In El Salvador, several females of its close relative the Banded Banner (*P. neaerea*) may lay their eggs on one shoot of a *Paullinia* vine, a relative of the Guaraná (*P. cupana*). The vine contains toxic alkaloids that may render both larvae and adults unpalatable (its caterpillars are nonetheless attacked by parasitic wasps). Adults do not visit flowers but feed on rotting fruit, tree wounds and dung.

▲ *Epiphile orea*, Manu National Park, Peru
The genus *Epiphile* contains some 15 species of mountain-forest butterflies. The Orea Banner (*Epiphile orea*) ranges from Argentina to Costa Rica, where it is an uncommon butterfly of the cloud forest and mountain passes. Males chase other butterflies from a favorite perch in the canopy; they apparently feed on nothing but fresh mammal dung or carrion. Females spend the morning in the canopy, then descend to the forest floor, where they are sometimes attracted to rotting fruits.

◄ *Callicore cynosura*, Tambopata National Reserve, Peru
◣ *Callicore atacama manova*, San Isidro, Costa Rica
Gemlike little *Callicore* butterflies are a common sight on moist ground in tropical American forests. Huge numbers are killed to make trinkets for the souvenir trade. They are attracted to human skin and often alight to sip sweat from visitors. There are 20 recognized species, though based on their caterpillars and molecular data some may belong in other genera. Like the eighty-eights, their underwing patterns have inspired imaginative English names; the "BD butterfly" (*Callicore cynosura*) of the Amazon, for example, seems to display those letters on its hindwings.

Emperors

The emperors (Apaturinae) are close relatives of the tropical brushfoots. They are stout-bodied, often colorful butterflies found practically worldwide, though 13 of the 20 genera are confined to southern and eastern Asia. Only two, *Doxocopa* and *Asterocampa* (the hackberry butterflies), live in the Americas.

Many apaturines are close mimics of other butterflies, in particular some of the Asian tigers (*Parantica* spp.). Their caterpillars feed largely on hackberries (*Celtis* spp.) and related plants. About 27 million years ago, however, butterflies in the genus *Apatura* switched to plants in the willow family. This was not an easy move, because willows contain a chemical, salicin, that is toxic to caterpillars; the butterflies had to evolve a defense against it before they could tolerate their new hosts.

▶ *Euripus nyctelius*, Cameron Highlands, West Malaysia

The Courtesan (*Euripus nyctelius*) is a butterfly of lowland primary rainforest in Southeast Asia. Males mimic a milkweed butterfly, the Magpie Crow (*Euploea rhadamanthus*). Females are larger and copy either the male or female Magpie Crow, with numerous intermediates. The females have more rounded hindwings than the males and, unlike the strongly flying males, copy the slow, unhurried flight of their model. Both sexes have golden yellow eyes. They lay their eggs on species of *Trema*, a tree in the elm family (Ulmaceae).

▶ *Doxocopa laurentia cherubina*, Risaralda, Colombia

The Turquoise Emperor (*Doxocopa laurentia*) is one of 15 tropical American butterflies in *Doxocopa*. This is a male. The female has a broad white wing band topped with orange. It resembles, and perhaps mimics, some of the sisters (*Adelpha* spp.). Turquoise Emperors live in lower-elevation cloud forests from Mexico to Paraguay. Females usually stay high in the canopy, but males drop to the ground to feed on rotting fruit and damp soil. The northern Andean race *D. l. cherubina*, shown here, is sometimes considered a separate species.

▲◄ *Apatura iris*, Switzerland
The Purple Emperor (*Apatura iris*), one of the most sought-after of European butterflies, is famed for the purple sheen on the upperwings of the male. It ranges from central Europe east to China and Korea. Emperors spend much of their time high in trees, and several males may gather in the tallest oak in the vicinity. When a female arrives, the dominant male gives chase, fending off his rivals and following her, sometimes for as much as 500 m (1,600 ft), before mating.

Mapwings and Daggerwings

The Cyrestinae is a small subfamily with a wide distribution. Two of its three genera, the mapwings (*Cyrestis*) and the Southeast Asian maplets (*Chersonesia*), live in the Old World tropics. The third, the daggerwings (*Marpesia*), is confined to the Americas.

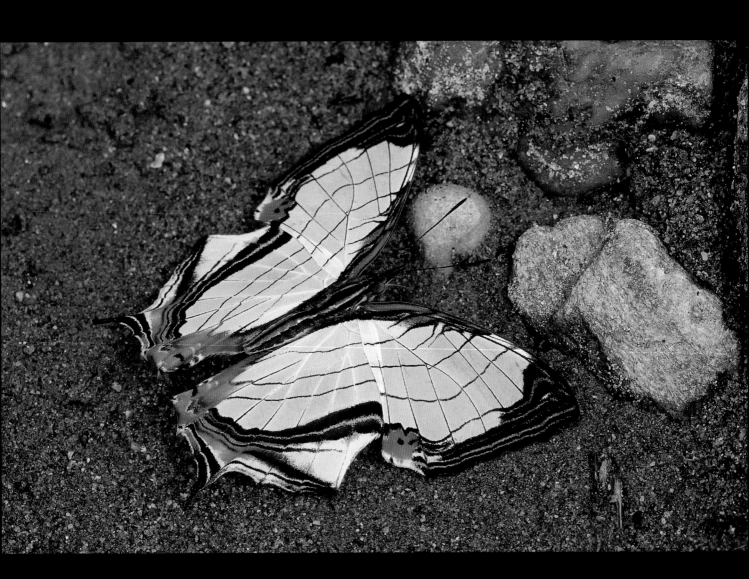

▲ *Cyrestis nivea*, Tambunan, Sabah, Malaysia
The 20 mapwings, named for the fine pattern of lines on their upper surface, range from Africa to New Guinea. The Straight-line Mapwing (*Cyrestis nivea*) lives in rainforests from Myanmar (Burma) to the Lesser Sundas. It usually flies high in trees or rests on the underside of a leaf; it is most often seen at forest edges or along streams or trails. The males, like those of other mapwings, often land on wet ground, where they may stay for some time, perching with open wings.

The fragile, slender tails on the hindwings of the 17 species of daggerwings recall swallowtails, but daggerwings have straight rather than recurved antennae and, like all nymphalids, four functional legs rather than six. Daggerwings are rapid and active in flight. They visit flowers regularly, and males frequently gather in numbers to seek mineral salts from moist earth. Their caterpillars carry two long spines on their heads and a row of shorter spines down the back.

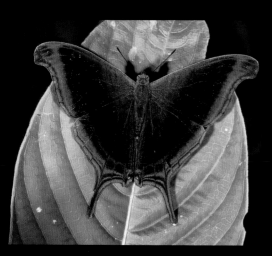

◄ *Marpesia zerynthia*, male, Manu National Park, Peru

The body and the basal half of the underside of the wings of the Waiter Daggerwing (*Marpesia zerynthia*) are as crisply white as a waiter's uniform. Waiter Daggerwings range from Mexico to Brazil and straggle occasionally into southern Texas. They occupy a broad range of elevations and habitats but are commonest in cloud forest. Males sometimes feed on dung and may gather in large numbers at puddles. Both sexes visit flowers of *Cordia* and *Croton* species, and adults often roost together, clinging to the undersides of leaves.

◄ *Marpesia furcula*, male, Risaralda, Colombia

The Glossy or Sunset Daggerwing (*Marpesia furcula*) occurs in two forms. This is the "iole" form, with a band of iridescent purple crossing its wings. One of the more spectacular daggerwings, this rainforest butterfly ranges from Nicaragua south to Argentina. Like some of its kin, this species occasionally emerges and migrates en masse, often in company with other butterflies. Though males regularly visit moist soil for mineral salts, females remain in the canopy and are rarely seen.

◄ *Marpesia petreus*, Yuto, Chocó, Colombia

The Ruddy Daggerwing (*Marpesia petreus*) is the most northerly of its genus. It flies all year in southern Florida, has bred in Texas and Arizona, and strays as far north as Kansas and Colorado. The species also ranges south to Brazil. Males watch for females from perches 5 to 10 m (16–33 ft) up in sunlit trees. Their orange-and-black caterpillars feed on species of fig (*Ficus*). Adults feed at flowers but also visit rotting fruit and wet soil. Their orange color may mimic the Julia Heliconian (*Dryas iulia*).

The ladies (Nymphalinae) are a worldwide subfamily of more than 500 species, including some of the world's best-known and most widely distributed butterflies. They range across every continent but Antarctica and have reached many oceanic islands. One of only two native butterflies in the Hawaiian Islands, the Kamehameha butterfly (*Vanessa tameamea*), belongs to this group. It is Hawaii's official state insect but, like many Hawaiian animals, is in decline. The subfamily is divided into six tribes, plus a few species that do not seem to fit into any of them. One tribe, the Kallimini, includes the remarkable Asian leaf butterflies (*Kallima* spp.), the most perfect leaf-mimics in the butterfly world.

▶ *Baeotus beotus*, Risaralda, Colombia

The Coeini contains only six species in two genera (*Baeotus* and *Historis*) that are confined to tropical America. The Beotus Beauty (*Baeotus beotus*) is a butterfly of the rainforest canopy. Its upperwings are black, crossed with an iridescent blue band. It ranges from Costa Rica to the Amazon, though some of its forms may be better placed with related species. *Baeotus* butterflies do not visit flowers but feed instead on rotting fruit. Males perch on tree trunks.

Ladies, Commas and Others
Tribe Nymphalini

The tribe Nymphalini, with about 100 species, is worldwide in distribution and includes some of the best-known butterflies of the north temperate zone. Temperate species usually hibernate as adults and are among the earliest butterflies to appear in spring.

◄ ▲ *Vanessa cardui*, Switzerland

The Painted Lady (*Vanessa cardui*), one of 19 species in the genus *Vanessa*, is the most widely distributed butterfly in the world. It is found on every continent except South America and Antarctica. It is also one of the best-known butterfly migrants, regularly crossing the Mediterranean between North Africa and Europe; it also flies, sometimes in huge numbers, from Mexico as far north as Canada. Its caterpillars feed on more than 100 species of plants, though both larvae and nectar-seeking adults have a preference for thistles.

◄ *Vanessa atalanta*, Switzerland

The Red Admiral (*Vanessa atalanta*) is widespread, adaptable and an accomplished migrant. Found across the northern hemisphere, it has also been introduced into Hawaii and New Zealand. In North and Central America it is widespread in open habitats south to Guatemala. Though the adults hibernate, in hard winters most northern butterflies die and must be replaced by migrants from the south. Its larvae feed primarily on plants in the nettle family (Urticaceae). The caterpillar makes a tent for itself by folding a nettle leaf, emerging only to feed.

▶ *Nymphalis antiopa*, Switzerland

Nymphalis antiopa is called Mourning Cloak in North America and Camberwell Beauty in Britain, where it is a rare wanderer. It ranges across most of the temperate northern hemisphere. Adults hibernate, usually beneath loose bark. In eastern North America they may emerge as early as February to feed on running sap. Mourning Cloaks bask in the sun on cool days; their dark color helps them take up heat. Adults can live for 10 months but die soon after mating and egg-laying in spring.

▶ *Polygonia c-album*, Switzerland

The Comma (*Polygonia c-album*) is named for a white comma-shaped mark on the underside of the hindwing. It is a butterfly of temperate Eurasia and North Africa, though it has close relatives in North America. It hibernates over winter among dead leaves, camouflaged by its mottled brown underside and irregular shape. In spring the awakened adults produce a second brood that lives until autumn, giving rise in turn to the generation that will hibernate during the following winter.

▶ *Aglais urticae*, Switzerland

The Small Tortoiseshell (*Aglais urticae*) is generally common across temperate Eurasia but has declined in some areas. In Britain this decline has been blamed on a recent invader, the parasitic fly *Sturmia bella*. Small Tortoiseshells produce one or two broods a year, with autumn adults hibernating until spring. Males set up territories in patches of nettles, their larval food plant. When a female arrives, the male perches behind her and strikes her hindwings repeatedly with his antennae. This courtship may be repeated for hours before the couple finally mate.

Peacocks, Pages and Others

Tribe Victorinini

The tribe Victorinini includes four tropical American genera, with some species ranging into warmer parts of the temperate zone. Their nearest relative is the African Leaf Butterfly (*Kallimoides rumia*), a tropical African species once thought to be closer to the Asian leaf butterflies (*Kallima* spp.).

◄ *Anartia amathea*, Auberge des Orp., French Guiana

The Scarlet Peacock or Coolie (*Anartia amathea*) is an often abundant butterfly from Central and northern South America, including some of the Lesser Antilles. In Trinidad it may be the commonest butterfly, particularly at the start of the rains, when flowers are in bloom. Adults live only about two weeks. This is a male; in females the red is replaced by a dull orange. Experiments have shown that the male's colored band has no effect on a female's choice; instead it may warn away predators.

◄ *Anartia jatrophae*, Saül, French Guiana

The White Peacock (*Anartia jatrophae*) is the most widespread of the five species of *Anartia*. It is common in open, sunny habitats in Florida, breeds in south Texas, and wanders as far as Nebraska, New Mexico and North Carolina. It is also found throughout the West Indies and as far south as Argentina. Its caterpillars feed on Water Hyssop (*Bacopa moniera*) and other plants. Adults are often found along streams and drainage ditches, but they may leave seemingly suitable areas if flowers are not in bloom.

▶ *Metamorpha elissa*, Tingo Maria, Peru

The Elissa Page (*Metamorpha elissa*), the only member of its genus, is a forest butterfly found from Panama to Bolivia. It can be found up to 1,200 m (4,000 ft) in rainforest, deciduous forest and cloud forest. Its upper side is mostly dark brownish black, crossed with a broad white band that breaks up into spots on the forewing, with a narrower orange band below it. Adults visit flowers such as Lantana, and males may alight on wet sand, where they are extremely wary.

▶ *Siproeta epaphus*, Manu National Park, Peru

The Rusty-tipped Page (*Siproeta epaphus*), one of three species in the genus *Siproeta*, ranges from Mexico to Peru and occasionally straggles into south Texas or New Mexico. It is usually found in disturbed situations, though in Costa Rica it prefers montane forest. Males patrol forest edges or stream cuts or wait for females from a perch, driving rivals from their territories. These butterflies have been seen migrating in numbers in southern Ecuador, accompanying a large swarm of Purple-washed Skippers (*Panoquina sylvicola*) and unidentified darner dragonflies (Family Aeshnidae).

▶ *Siproeta stelenes*, Manu National Park, Peru

The Malachite (*Siproeta stelenes*), the best-known and most-widespread species of *Siproeta*, is resident from Argentina and Bolivia north to southern Florida (where it apparently arrived from Cuba in the 1960s) and the extreme south of Texas. It has also strayed as far north as Kansas. Adults feed mostly on rotting fruit, though they will visit other food sources, from flowers to animal dung. Largely a butterfly of secondary growth, it closely resembles (and may mimic) the Dido Longwing (*Philaethria dido*), a tropical rainforest species.

Buckeyes and Pansies
Tribe Junoniini

The tribe Junoniini contains only six genera but includes such familiar butterflies as the buckeyes of the Americas and the pansies of the Old World (both now in *Junonia*). It also includes the Old World eggflies (*Hypolimnas* spp.), a group that includes mimics of a number of milkweed butterflies (Danaiini).

▲ *Junonia orithya*, **Niah National Park, Sarawak, Malaysia**
The 34 species of *Junonia* are found almost worldwide. The Blue or Eyed Pansy (*Junonia orithya*) is an open-country butterfly that is widespread in fields and gardens. It is common in open places throughout much of Africa, southern Asia and Australia. Males may have more of the brilliant blue on the hindwings that gives the Blue Pansy its common name, but the females compensate with larger eyespots and expanded orange bars on the forewing. Blue Pansies often perch with their wings open, basking

The 25 or so genera in the tribe Melitaeini include the crescents (*Phycoides* and *Anthanassa* spp.) and checkerspots (*Chlosyne, Euphydryas* and related genera), as well as a number of tropical American butterflies. Most genera in the Melitaeini are confined to the Americas. The genus *Melitaea* itself, however, with more than 80 species – many confusingly called fritillaries – is temperate Eurasian and North African, with one species in Ethiopia. It reaches its highest diversity in central Asia.

▶ *Melitaea athalia*, Switzerland

The Heath Fritillary (*Melitaea athalia*) is a butterfly of heath, woodland clearings and grasslands. Widespread in temperate Eurasia as far east as Japan, it is very rare in Britain. It is extremely variable in both color and pattern. Larvae feed on plants from a number of different families, including plantains (*Plantago* spp.). Heath Fritillaries require a well-connected series of habitat patches; they have declined in many parts of Europe as changes in forest management have reduced the number of suitable clearings.

▶ *Melitaea didyma*, Switzerland

The Spotted Fritillary (*Melitaea didyma*) is a common and widespread butterfly of hot, dry, grassy meadows and flowery roadsides in central and southern Europe, North Africa, the Middle East and central Asia. Its caterpillars feed on plantains (*Plantago* spp.), violets (*Viola* spp.), toadflax (*Linaria* spp.) and other plants. Males bask in sheltered bare hollows while waiting for females to pass by. At night both sexes roost on flower heads, but if rain threatens they will retreat deep into the grass tussocks.

◢ *Anthanassa crithona*, Chiripo National Park, Costa Rica

The 16 species of *Anthanassa* are common in forest clearings, pastures and disturbed areas in tropical America. Two, the Texan Crescent (*A. texana*) and the Cuban Crescent (*A. frisia*), reach the southern United States, and others stray there occasionally. The Orange-banded Crescent (*A. crithona*) lives on wet mountain slopes from Nicaragua to Panama, where it flies along forest edges. Larvae of other *Anthanassa* species feed largely on members of the acanthus family (Acanthaceae), including the Shrimp Plant (*Beloperone guttata*).

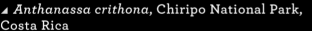

The Lycaenidae include what is probably the tiniest of butterflies, the Western Pygmy Blue (*Brephidium exilis*), which has a wingspan of only 1.2 to 2 cm (0.5–0.75 in). It ranges from the western United States to Venezuela. There are between 5,000 and 6,000 lycaeinid species, making this the second largest butterfly family. They are generally small, usually are less than 5 cm (2 in) across. Most are eager nectar-feeders. Male lycaenids have fused joints and missing claws on their forelimbs, but the forelimbs of females are normal. Both sexes, unlike nymphalids and male metalmarks, walk on all six legs.

Lycaenid caterpillars are stubby and slug-shaped and look quite different from those of most other butterflies. Many pass their larval lives in close association with ants, feeding them on secretions in return for protection, a relationship known as myrmecophily.

The Lycaenidae has been divided into seven sub-families. One of the oddest, the Miletinae, includes the Harvester (*Feniseca tarquinius*) of North America. Its caterpillars are, unusually, carnivorous, feeding on aphids or other insects.

▶ *Polyommatus dorylas*, Switzerland
The Turquoise Blue (*Polyommatus dorylas*, Subfamily Polyommatinae) lives in damp, flowery meadows over calcareous soils, from near sea level to as high as 2,300 m (7,500 ft). It ranges across southern Europe and east to the Urals and the Caucasus. It has two broods a year in lowlands but only one at higher elevations. Turquoise Blue caterpillars feed on Kidney Vetch (*Anthyllis vulneraria*) and are attended by the ant species *Lasius alienus*, *Myrmica scabrinodis* and *Formica cinerea*. This is the only European blue with broad white borders and orange chevrons on its underwings.

Hairstreaks (subfamily Theclinae) are extremely diverse, with 18 recognized tribes. They are found almost worldwide outside the polar regions and are particularly varied in eastern Asia. Hairstreaks fly rapidly and erratically and usually perch with their wings closed. They take their name from either the fine streaks on their underwings or the hair-like tails on their hindwings, though some species lack either. Hairstreak tails are often combined with eyespots; the result may look enough like an insect's head, complete with antennae, to fool a predator. This "false head" illusion is heightened by the actions of the butterfly, which saws its hindwings back and forth, causing the fake antennae to wiggle.

◄ *Satyrium w-album*, Switzerland
The White-letter Hairstreak (*Satyrium w-album*, Tribe Eumaeini) takes its English and scientific names from the W-shaped white line on the underside of its hindwing. Except when feeding at flowers or chasing other butterflies, it sits quietly high in the treetops. Though found across Eurasia, this is a highly sedentary butterfly that lives in small colonies centered around clumps of elms (*Ulmus* spp.), its only larval food plant. White-letter Hairstreaks declined severely in Britain after the outbreak of Dutch elm blight in 1976.

◄ *Eumaeus minyas*, Tambopata National Reserve, Peru
Eumaeus (Tribe Eumaeini) is a genus of five tailless, colorful tropical American hairstreaks whose caterpillars feed on cycads (*Zamia* spp.). Best known is the Atala (*E. atala*), which has regained its numbers in southeastern Florida with the increased popularity of cycads in gardens. *Eumaeus* caterpillars take up a toxic alkaloid, cycasin, from their host plants, and both larvae and adults are unpalatable; the adult's bright colors probably serve as a warning. The Minyas Cycadian (*E. minyas*) ranges from Colombia to Peru and central Brazil.

◄ *Evenus felix*, Baños, Ecuador
Evenus felix, one of a dozen tropical American *Evenus* species, is a highly colored, iridescent Andean butterfly. The bright green of its underwings may camouflage it against a sunlit leaf. Dealers in Baños, eastern Ecuador, have been ranching specimens for at least a century for sale to collectors under the name *Evenus coronata*, which now applies to the Crowned Hairstreak, an extremely similar Central and South American species. *Evenus* butterflies lay eggs on plants in the sapodilla family (Sapotaceae), among the few lycaenids to do so.

▶ *Hypochrysops pythias*, Crater Mountain, Papua New Guinea

The Peacock Jewel (*Hypochrysops pythias*, Tribe Luciini) of the lowland rainforests of Papua New Guinea and tropical Queensland, Australia, is part of a large, almost entirely Australasian genus. It sometimes appears in hundreds when its host tree, *Commersonia bartramia*, is in regrowth. Numbers of both sexes may cluster together on a leaf. Larvae shelter on the undersides of leaves; they pupate inside a rolled leaf or among dead leaves on the ground. Males like this one are iridescent blue above and fly high in the forest canopy.

▶ *Zeltus amasa*, Taman Negara, Malaysia

A number of Southeast Asian hairstreaks, in several genera scattered among different tribes, share impressively long, silky white tails and underside patterns of orange and white flecked with black. This one, the Fluffy Tit (*Zeltus amasa*, Tribe Hypolycaenini), is common in lowland rain-forests from India and southern China to Java and the Philippines. Adults prefer open, sunny spots where they can bask with open wings. Males perch on top of leaves or visit patches of damp soil; they will feed on bird droppings.

▶ *Drupadia ravindra*, Tanjung Puting National Park, Kalimantan, Indonesia

Only some subspecies of the Common Posy (*Drupadia ravindra*, Tribe Cheritrini) have a bright orange bar on the upper side of the forewing. *Drupadia* butterflies show much individual variation. The males of many species come in two forms, either colorful or smaller, duller and more like their females; females can be variable too. The Common Posy is common in forests from Myanmar and Indochina south to Java and east to the Philippines. It has a slow, flitting flight, and often returns to the same perch.

Coppers

The coppers and their relatives (subfamily Lycaeninae) include nine genera that are mostly confined to Eurasia and North America, though one species lives in Guatemala and two in New Guinea. Of the nearly 60 coppers (*Lycaena* spp.), all but six are butterflies of the temperate northern hemisphere. Four live in New Zealand and two in South Africa. Unlike hairstreaks, coppers often bask with their wings open.

▲ *Lycaena virgaureae*, Alps, Switzerland

The Scarce Copper (*Lycaena virgaureae*) is not really scarce, except in Britain – where it may never have occurred at all. It ranges from Spain to Mongolia and is common in the Alps, the Pyrenees and other mountain areas. It lives in subalpine meadows, flowery pastures and other grassland areas between 600 and 2,000 m (2,000–6,500 ft). Males like this one are aggressively territorial, chasing off rivals from a perch on a flower head. Females lay their eggs on species of wood sorrel (*Rumex*).

▲ *Lycaena hippothoe eurydame*, Alps, Switzerland

The alpine race of the Purple-edged Copper (*Lycaena hippothoe eurydame*) lacks the purple edging that gives this species its name, but the male is colorful nonetheless. The species ranges from the Pyrenees to the Urals and the Altai range, usually in mountain foothills but at sea level in Scandinavia. It tends to live in small colonies in damp, flower-filled meadows or hillside bogs. Males defend territories of 10 to 20 square meters (107–215 sq ft) in patches of nectar-rich flowers, either by means of patrol flights or from a perch.

The blues (subfamily Polyommatinae) are the tiniest and daintiest of butterflies. They are very diverse: the subfamily contains 121 genera, and the single genus *Polyommatus* has more than 200 species. True to their name, most blues (the males, at least) are iridescent blue on the upper side of their wings. Flashes of blue from a flying male may signal females that a suitor is in the area. Blues are active insects that flutter busily among clumps of flowers. Males may gather at the edges of ponds or puddles, sometimes in the hundreds. Many blues are very local, and some are at great risk of extinction. The Xerces Blue (*Glaucopsyche xerces*), whose only habitat disappeared beneath the sprawling city of San Francisco, became completely extinct in about 1943. It posthumously gave its name to the Xerces Society for Invertebrate Conservation, one of the world's premier insect conservation organizations.

▶ *Nacaduba cyanea*, Daintree National Park, Queensland, Australia

The 43 species of *Nacaduba* range from India to Australia and Fiji. The Green-banded Line Blue (*N. cyanea*) is a rainforest-edge butterfly found in the Moluccas, New Guinea, the Solomon Islands and coastal northern Queensland, Australia. Adults are about 3 cm (1.2 in) across. Adult males are blue above, with a black border and a pale patch on the hindwing; females are black and white. Their bright green caterpillars feed on two species of sea bean (*Entada*) and are tended by ants of the genus *Anonychomyrma*.

▶ *Polyommatus damon*, Switzerland

The Damon Blue (*Polyommatus damon*) is a local single-brooded butterfly of nutrient-poor mountain grasslands from Spain to Mongolia. The pale stripe on the underside of its hindwing is distinctive. North of the Alps, the Damon Blue has declined rapidly as sainfoins (*Onychobrychis* spp.), its larval food plants, have been lost to mechanized agriculture and a drying climate. Because it lays eggs high on aging flower stalks, it is vulnerable to grazing and mowing. Its caterpillars feed late in the afternoon, often attended by ants of the genera *Lasius* or *Formica*.

The metalmarks (Riodinidae) are a family of small, often brilliantly colored, mostly tropical butterflies. They get their name from the silvery flecks that decorate the wings of many species. Metalmarks are active butterflies. They generally prefer sunny patches in forests, and although they visit flowers, adults also get nutrients from carrion. Although metalmarks are found almost throughout the world, by far the largest number – all, in fact, but around 100 of the more than 1,400 known species – live in the New World tropics.

Fossil metalmarks have been found preserved in 25-million-year-old Dominican amber. Today the Riodinidae is often included within the Lycaenidae rather than as a family on its own. Morphological and genetic studies suggest that the two families are each other's closest relatives. Like nymphalids and some male lycaenids, metalmark males have reduced forelimbs; also like lycaenids, the caterpillars of some species are attended by ants.

The family is divided into three subfamilies. One, the Nemeobiinae, includes all the metalmarks in the Old World. The other two, the Euselasiinae and the Riodininae, are confined to the Americas.

▲ *Paralaxita damajanti*, Danum Valley Conservation Area, Sabah, Malaysia
◄ *Paralaxita telesia*, Harau Canyon, Sumatra, Indonesia

Paralaxita includes four species of Southeast Asian metalmarks with carmine-red underparts flecked with black and metallic blue. These metalmarks are generally uncommon. Though attractive and colorful, they can be difficult to see, as they fly low and keep to the depths of heavy forest. The Malayan Red Harlequin (*Paralaxita damajanti*) lives in southern Thailand, peninsular Malaysia, Sumatra and Borneo. The Red Harlequin (*Paralaxita telesia*) has a similar range but also extends to Indochina.

◄ *Hamearis lucina*, Switzerland

The Duke of Burgundy (*Hamearis lucina*), sometimes called a fritillary, is the only metalmark in Europe and the sole member of its genus. It ranges in scattered colonies as far east as the Urals, preferring open woodland and grasslands on chalk and limestone soils, where it can find its two main larval food plants, Cowslip (*Primula veris*) and Primrose (*P. vulgaris*). It overwinters as a pupa, hidden beneath a dead leaf on the ground and attached to its food plant by a silken girdle.

► *Abisara rogersi*, Kibale National Park, Uganda

The *Abisara* butterflies of Africa and tropical Asia are collectively known as judies. (Members of the related genus *Dodona* are called punches, or punchinellos, and other Asian metalmarks are called columbines and harlequins.) The Light-banded Judy (*Abisara rogersi*), one of only 11 metalmarks in continental Africa, is found from Nigeria and Uganda south to Angola and Zambia. It prefers the shadier parts of the forest, though it may occur in open forest in submontane areas.

The dazzling diversity of shapes, sizes and colors exhibited by the tropical American metalmarks is unmatched by any other butterfly group. Many, particularly females, are mimics, and the range of butterflies (and day-flying moths) they copy is also unequaled in other butterfly families. Many species are local, rare and little known. Where they do occur, they may be very particular about their perching sites (where groups of males gather to await passing females), occupying the same areas year after year and visiting them only at select times of the day.

◄ *Helicopis cupido*, Leticia, Colombia
Helicopis contains three species of metalmarks with impressive tails on their hindwings. The Spangled Cupid (*H. cupido*) Is a lowland rainforest butterfly of northern South America, commonest between 200 and 300 m (660–985 ft). It is usually found perching under leaves in marshy areas, including the borders of forest lagoons. Groups of more than 20 larvae and pupae have been found inside single rolled-up leaves of *Montrichardia*, a member of the arum family (Araceae).

◄ *Lasaia arsis*, Iguaçu National Park, Brazil
The Cat's-eye Sapphire (*Lasaia arsis*) is one of 14 metalmarks in the genus *Lasaia*. It is found in Ecuador, Peru, Brazil and northern Argentina; a relative, the Blue Metalmark (*L. sula*), reaches the extreme south of Texas. Males of *Lasaia* are highly iridescent blue or bluish above, spotted with black, while the rarely seen females tend to be brownish. They are fast and erratic fliers. Male Cat's-eye Sapphires are active in sunny weather, flying close to the ground and alighting frequently on moist sandbanks.

▲ *Chorinea sylphina terpsichore*, Coroico, Bolivia

▶ *Chorinea sylphina*, Manu National Park, Peru

The eight species of *Chorinea* are among the most striking of butterflies, recalling the dragontails (*Lamproptera* spp.) of eastern Asia. The Sylphina Angel (*Chorinea sylphina*) tends to stay in the canopy, flying or perching on the undersides of leaves, although males will seek mineral salts on the ground. This is a cloud-forest butterfly, usually found between 2,000 and 3,000 m (6,600–9,850 ft) in the mountains of Ecuador, Peru and Bolivia. It can extend a small yellow bladder from its thorax, but we do not yet know why.

▶ *Rhetus arcius huanus*, Tingo Maria, Peru

The Long-tailed Metalmark or Sword-tailed Doctor (*Rhetus arcius*) is one of three dazzling rainforest species in the genus *Rhetus*. It can be found at forest edges, along streams or in sunlit forest gaps from southern Mexico to Amazonian Peru. Males spend the early morning 3 to 8 m (10–25 ft) up on the undersides of leaves, chasing other insects or waiting for mates, but they descend later to feed from soil. Their caterpillars feed on two rainforest trees, *Terminalia amazonica* (Combretaceae family) and *Mabea occidentalis* (Euphorbiaceae family).

◀ *Rhetus dysonii*, Manu National Park, Peru

Dyson's Metalmark or Dyson's Blue Doctor (*Rhetus dysonii*) ranges from Panama to Bolivia and Brazil. It can be found along forested roadsides, on the banks of forest streams or in sunlit glades at elevations between 800 and 1,200 m (2,600–4,000 ft). It prefers dappled sunlight and is most active in the early afternoon. During dry weather it may visit streamside rocks to feed on bird droppings. Both sexes visit muddy soil, often accompanied by other butterflies, and show a preference for trees with small white flowers.

◀ *Eurybia lycisca*, Boraudo, Chocó, Colombia

Eurybia butterflies are moth-like insects that spend much of their time perching on the undersides of leaves in lowland rainforest. Their proboscis is one of the longest for their body size of any butterfly, one and a half times longer than their head and body combined. The pupa has an extended sheath that holds the proboscis as it grows. *Eurybia* caterpillars feed on gingers and related plants, apparently eating only the flower parts instead of the leaves. The Blue-winged Eurybia (*Eurybia lycisca*) ranges from southeastern Mexico to Bolivia.

◀ *Emesis fatimella*, Risaralda, Colombia

Emesis is a large genus of heavy-bodied, mostly brown or dull orange (occasionally purplish) butterflies, characteristically banded with wavy blackish lines, that range from the southwestern United States to Argentina. Two species reach Arizona and two more are rare strays into southern Texas. The Orange Tanmark or Noble Emesis (*Emesis fatimella*) is found from southern Mexico to the Guianas and Trinidad. In Costa Rica it is occasionally seen around midday, flying along forest edges or above streams. Both sexes visit plants with small white flowers.

▶ *Menander coruscans*, Coroico, Bolivia

The genus *Menander* includes 11 tropical forest species ranging from Mexico through Central and northern South America. Males are mostly black above, marked with iridescent blue. Their caterpillars are very unusual, protected by a broad, hard carapace like a turtle's shell that covers their legs and body. Ants tend them but – according to Philip deVries – "seldom enthusiastically." Adults are fast, erratic fliers whose wings make an audible whirring sound in flight. *Menander coruscans* is found in the Guianas, Brazil and Bolivia.

▶ *Semomesia capanaea*, Relais de Patawa, French Guiana

The Capanea Eyemark (*Semomesia capanaea*) lives east of the Andes in rainforests of the Amazon Basin and the Guiana Shield. *Semomesia* butterflies are generally known as eyemarks in recognition of the large eyespots on their forewings. Both sexes have the spots but females are otherwise generally brown, with a wide white band across the wings. Like other tropical metalmarks, the males are often seen in small groups and spend much of their time perched on the undersides of leaves. Females are encountered much more rarely.

An adult butterfly's task is to reproduce, and its wings are its reason for being. The color patterns they display may attract a mate, deter a rival, warn off a predator or conceal their owner from an enemy. Flight, because it carries adult butterflies far and wide, prevents inbreeding, provides the best chance to find a high-quality mate or the best place to lay eggs, and ensures that butterfly populations do not become localized and overcrowded. How butterflies fly is determined by their wing shape and size, but even more critically by their needs.

▶ *Ornithoptera priamus*, Lae, Papua New Guinea (Papilionidae: Papilioninae)
Fast, erratic flight may be a lifesaver for a butterfly being pursued by a bird, but unpalatable Common Tree Nymphs (*Idea stolli*) float slowly and gracefully, secure in their instinctive knowledge that predators will avoid them. The brilliant green-and-black pattern on a male Common Birdwing (Ornithoptera priamus) warns predators that it, too, is unpalatable.
▶▶ *Idea stolli*, Poring Hot Springs, Sabah, Malaysia (Nymphalidae: Danaiinae)

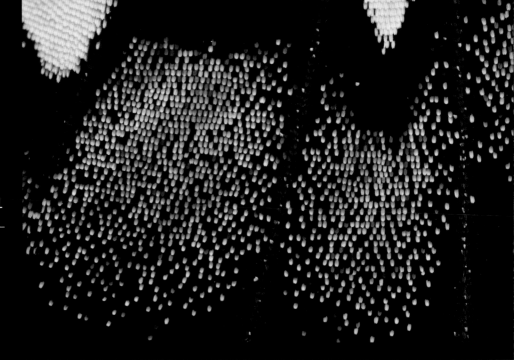

Color and Pattern

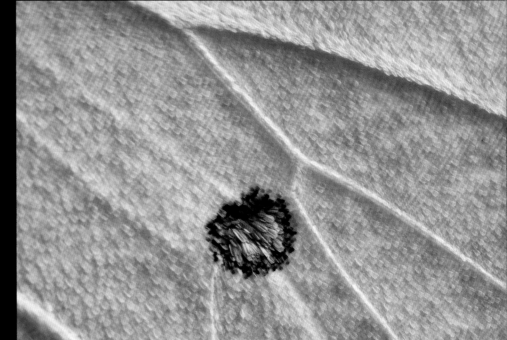

◥ *Papilio machaon*, Switzerland
(Papilionidae: Papilioninae)
▶ *Gonepteryx rhamni*, Switzerland
(Pieridae: Coliadinae)

Butterflies depend on their colors and patterns
to court mates, repel rivals and evade enemies.
Dark colors help basking butterflies absorb the
sun's heat, while whites reflect it away. Butterflies
get their color, and much of their pattern, from
the layers of scales that cover their wings. Scales
are tiny – no bigger than particles of dust – but
in these close-ups of the wings of an Old World
Swallowtail (*Papilio machaon*) and Brimstone
(*Gonepteryx rhamni*), you can see at least some
of them distinctly.

▲ *Actinote momina*, Manu National Park, Peru
(Nymphalidae: Heliconiinae)
▶ *Biblis hyperia*, Colombia (Nymphalidae: Biblidinae)
Not all butterflies are colorful, but the brightest of them have
dazzled human eyes for centuries. The startling reds of the Peru
Altinote (*Actinote momina*) and Red Rim (*Biblis hyperia*) come from
pigments packed into the scales covering the wing. Scientists have
yet to identify many of them, but the bright reds of heliconiine
longwings and swallowtails appear to be produced by different
pigments synthesized along differing genetic pathways.

▶ *Hebomoia leucippe*, Malaysia (captive) (Pieridae:
Coliadinae)
The colors in the wing scales of pierid butterflies result from both
pigments and structural elements. Pierid scales contain tiny oval
beads loaded with pterins, a family of pigments first discovered in
butterfly wings. Pterins absorb light, including ultraviolet, and the
beads scatter wavelengths that the pigments do not absorb. The
more densely the beads are packed, the more light they reflect and
the brighter the colors appear. The result can be brilliant, as on
the forewing of this Vibrant Sulphur (*Hebomoia leucippe*) from the
Moluccas.

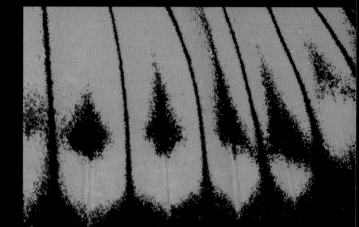

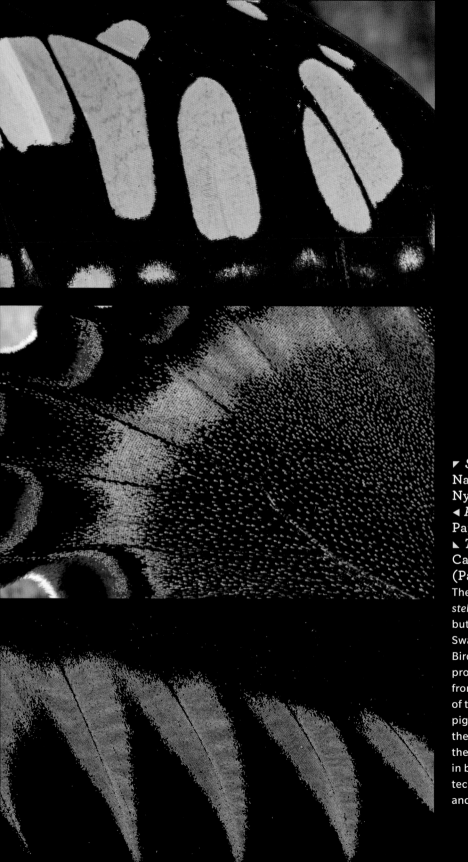

▼ *Siproeta stelenes*, Manu National Park, Peru (Nymphalidae: Nymphalinae)

◄ *Papilio maackii*, China (Papilionidae: Papioninae)

◣ *Trogonoptera brookiana*, Cameron Highlands, West Malaysia (Papilionidae: Papilioninae)

The rich greens of the Malachite (*Siproeta stelenes*) are probably produced by pigments, but the blues and greens of the Alpine Black Swallowtail (*Papilio maackii*) and Rajah Brooke's Birdwing (*Trogonoptera brookiana*) are structural, produced not by pigment but by light refracting from the intricately sculpted upper surfaces of their scales. Blacks are based on melanin pigments, but scale structure contributes to their intensity. Recently scientists have studied the mechanisms that produce structural colors in butterflies with an eye to their use in human technology, including the design of solar cells and anticounterfeiting patterns on banknotes.

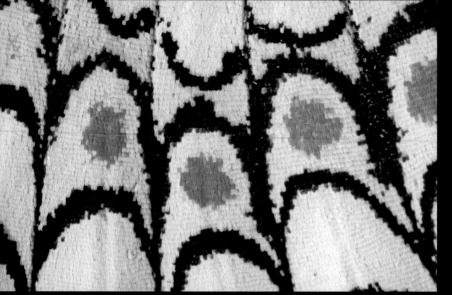

▼ *Melitaea phoebe*, Switzerland (Nymphalidae: Nymphalinae)
◄ *Siproeta stelenes*, Manu National Park, Peru (Nymphalidae: Nymphalinae)
▲ *Polyura athamas*, Gunung Leuser National Park, Sumatra, Indonesia (Nymphalidae: Charaxinae)
◣ *Cethosia biblis*, Malaysia (captive) (Nymphalidae: Heliconiinae)

The complicated wing patterns of brush-footed butterflies are apparently derived from an ancestral arrangement of bars, bands and spots in which each element has been modified, varied or eliminated over time. This basic nymphalid ground plan (NGP) has produced the complex arrays on the underwings of the Knapweed Fritillary (*Melitaea phoebe*) and Red Lacewing (*Cethosia biblis*), the brilliant colors of the Malachite (*Siproeta stelenes*) and Common Nawab (*Polyura athamas*), and even the remarkable dead-leaf patterns of Asian leaf mimics.

▲ *Zerynthia polyxena*, Padan Plain, Italy
(Papilionidae: Parnassiinae)
▶ *Polyura eudamippus*, Khao Yai National Park,
Thailand (Nymphalidae: Charaxinae)
Butterfly and moth wings display a greater variety of shapes
than is found in any other insect order. The shape affects their
aerodynamic properties, increases the insects' resemblance to
dead leaves or pieces of bark, and helps models resemble their
mimics. Shape and pattern work together: the scalloped wing
margins of the Southern Festoon (*Zerynthia polyxena*) and the
Great Nawab (*Polyura eudamippus*) enhance the ornamental
effect of their undulating bands of color.

▲ *Papilio paris*, Khao Yai National Park, Thailand (Papilionidae: Papilioninae)

◀ ▶ *Papilio machaon*, Switzerland (Papilionidae: Papilioninae)

Wings begin as buds within the caterpillar's body. A central area becomes the main part of the wing and a border strip forms its edge. In Lepidoptera this border is broader than in other insects, and apparently under separate genetic control. The "molecular cookie cutter" – a complex of genes and proteins that directs growth in the wing mar-

Eyespots

Caligo atreus, La Selva, Costa Rica
(Nymphalidae: Satyrinae)
This Yellow-edged Giant Owl (*Caligo atreus*)
might be hard to see were it not for its enormous
eyespots. Eyespots are butterfly defense mechanisms. Small ones, like those along the margins of
many satyrine wings, may lure a bird to the wrong
end of the butterfly, while large eyespots may
startle it. Some scientists have argued that this is
all they do, but more recent studies suggest that
if eyespots really look like the eyes of a larger animal, they may scare predators away altogether.

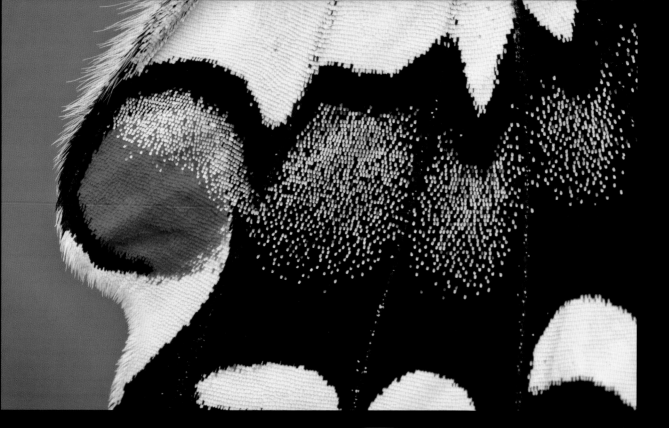

▲ *Papilio machaon*, Switzerland (Papilionidae: Papilioninae)

Eyespots don't have to be frightening to be useful. The red spot on the wing margin of an Old World Swallowtail (*Papilio machaon*) may not look like an eye, but it may get a predator's attention all the same. If a bird is attracted to the spot and attacks it, the butterfly may suffer only a torn wing. Some butterflies with conspicuous markings have wings that tear more easily than those of plainer species, suggesting that ditching a bit of wing may help its owner escape.

▶◢ *Morpho helenor*, Manu National Park, Peru (Nymphalidae: Satyrinae)

Do predators really mistake eyespots for eyes? Almost all well-developed eyespots, such as the ones on the undersides of the forewing (right) and hindwing (lower right) of this Common Morpho (*Morpho helenor*), contain a white "sparkle" in the center that resembles the highlight in a real three-dimensional vertebrate eye. In one experiment, birds appeared less likely to attack models if the sparkle was placed where it would be in a real eye, suggesting that it really is their resemblance to an eye that makes large eyespots valuable to butterflies.

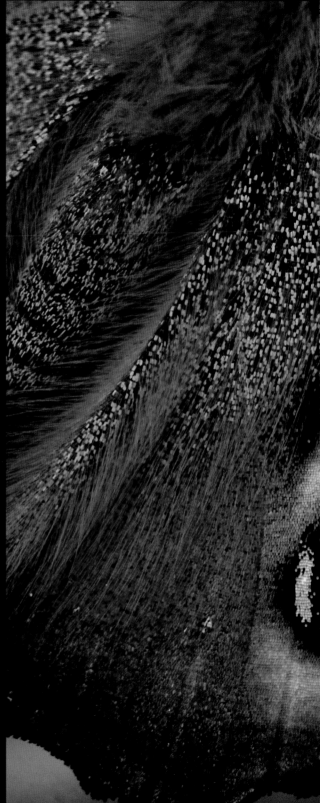

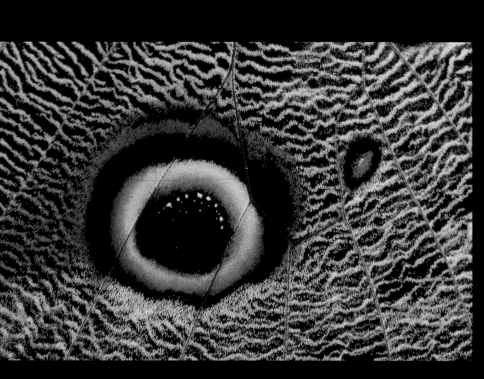

▲ *Caligo eurilochus*, Tambopata National Reserve, Peru (Nymphalidae: Satyrinae)

An eyespot may work because small birds (and perhaps other predators) have an innate fear of large, staring eyes. Birds may see the crescent-shaped "sparkle" in the eyespot of this Forest Giant Owl (*Caligo eurilochus*) differently from the way we do. Birds see in the ultraviolet range, and under ultraviolet light the sparkle appears much larger. Most, if not all, of the eyespot sparkles in butterflies reflect in the ultraviolet; they may have evolved in response to attacks from birds.

▶ *Aglais [Inachis] io*, Switzerland (Nymphalidae: Nymphalinae)

If a resting or hibernating European Peacock (*Aglais io*) is disturbed, it flicks its wings open, flashing four impressive eyespots, and makes ultrasonic hissing sounds that scare off mice, which are major predators of hibernating Peacocks. The suddenly revealed eyespots are not only startling but scary. Domestic chickens have reacted to them with alarm calls and nervous behavior, as though a predator were nearby. Wing flicks from butterflies with their eyespots painted over, however, startled the birds but didn't frighten them.

Sexual Dimorphism

▸ ◂ *Polyommatus bellargus* female (above), and male (below), Switzerland (Lycaenidae: Polyommatinae)
The males and females of many butterflies differ in color. Males, such as the male Adonis Blue (*Polyommatus bellargus*), are more likely to sport bright colors that attract females or (as probably happens more often) warn off rival males. Charles Darwin argued that sexual selection drove male evolution toward brighter and more distinctive color patterns, while the females – normally under less pressure to compete for mates – remained more conservative (though some male butterflies do select females by color). For many butterflies, Darwin's explanation seems correct.

▲ *Trogonoptera brookiana*, Cameron Highlands, West Malaysia (Papilionidae: Papilioninae) [male above, female below]
Alfred Russel Wallace, however, noticed that females are not always dull-colored. Females, particularly female birdwings, are often larger than males, and continental female Rajah Brooke's Birdwings (*Trogonoptera brookiana*) carry a white wing banner that is missing in the male. Wallace noted that in many swallowtails the females mimic other butterflies but the males – which may need to remain recognizable to females and rivals – do not. He proposed that sometimes it is the female's appearance that has changed most from that of her ancestors. For mimetic swallowtails in particular, he appears to have been right.

The life history of butterflies, passing from egg to larva (or caterpillar) to pupa and adult, is utterly alien to our own. Butterflies and caterpillars are so different from each other that we sometimes forget that they are stages of the same creature. Our mental image of a caterpillar as a baby butterfly, conjuring up images of our own young, is misleading: it is better to think of the caterpillar as a growth stage, and the 'adult' (more properly called the imago) as an often short-lived reproductive stage. The other two stages of a butterfly's life cycle, the egg and pupa, are required for development, and for extreme bodily change.

Adult butterflies do not pair-bond or care for their young. Males are constantly on the watch for females, either on patrolling flights or from a perch. Males and virgin females of some butterflies gather to mate on hilltops. After mating the sexes go their separate ways, the males to seek other mates and the females either to lay their fertilized eggs or, depending on the butterfly, to mate again.

▶ *Melanargia galathea*, Switzerland (Nymphalidae: Satyrinae)
The brown-and-cream underside of a mating female Marbled White (*Melanargia galathea*) contrasts prettily with the crisp gray and white of her partner.

Courtship and Mating

▲ *Pyrgus malvae*, Switzerland (Hesperiidae: Pyrginae)

Pyrgus skippers look much alike. Courting males release a variety of pheromones from androconial scales in a fold of the forewing, tufts of hairs on their legs, and patches of scales on their bodies. So far, 125 pheromones have been identified in nine *Pyrgus* species, including the Grizzled Skipper (*Pyrgus malvae*). Each species releases a unique pheromone cocktail that distinguishes it from others in the same area. Females may rely on these chemical signals to identify the right male.

◄ *Astraptes "fulgerator"*, Amacayacu National Park, Colombia (Hesperiidae: Pyrginae)

For butterflies to mate successfully, they must find a partner of their own species. We still do not know how many of them do it. These mating skippers are a case in point: they appear to be Two-barred Flashers (*Astraptes fulgerator*), butterflies that range from Texas to Argentina, but *fulgerator* now appears to be a complex of several nearly identical coexisting species (how many is still unknown). Only their caterpillars and host plants differ. How does a courting butterfly tell which is which?

▶ *Leptidea sinapis*, Switzerland
(Pieridae: Dismorphiinae)

Wood Whites (*Leptidea sinapis*) have unique court-ship rituals. A male will not try to mate until the female accepts him, and he might spend half an hour convincing her. As the two face each other, the male swings his white-tipped antennae and uncoiled proboscis back and forth in front of her. Wood Whites flick their wings open while courting, but the nearly identical Réal's and Cryptic Wood Whites (*L. reali* and *L. juvernica*) do not. The differ-ence may help females ensure that they are choos-ing the right species.

▶ *Boloria selene*, Switzerland
(Nymphalidae: Heliconiinae)

The Silver-bordered or Small Pearl-bordered Fritillary (*Boloria selene*) is a fast-flying butterfly found in marshes, wet meadows and bogs across the northern hemisphere. A male seeking a mate patrols low over potential breeding sites. When he finds a female, they mate quickly and stay hidden in low vegetation.

◄ *Plebejus idas*, Switzerland (Lycaenidae: Polyommatinae)

◣ *Polyommatus thersites*, Switzerland (Lycaenidae: Polyommatinae)

◥ *Polyommatus pylaon*, Switzerland (Lycaenidae: Polyommatinae)

➤ *Polyommatus coridon*, Switzerland (Lycaenidae: Polyommatinae)

Several European blues, including the Idas (*Plebejus idas*), Chapman's (*Polyommatus thersites*), Zephyr (*P. pylaon*) and Chalkhill Blues (*P. coridon*), may occur together. When a female makes her short flight to draw an acceptable male's attention, slight differences in color probably allow her to recognize his species. At close range, his pheromones may identify him. A male cannot recognize a female's underside pattern in the same way that humans do, but if she flies only for her own species he may not need to recognize her at all.

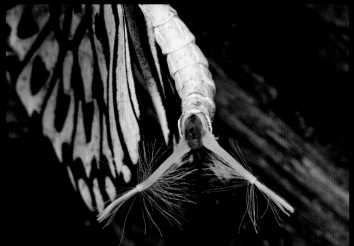

◀▲ *Idea leuconoe*, Philippines (Nymphalidae: Danaiinae)

As a male Siam Tree Nymph or Rice Paper Butterfly (*Idea leuconoe*) hovers over a female, he extrudes two pairs of brush-like "hair pencils" from his abdomen. The hair pencils release a cocktail of alkaloids, aromatic compounds and hydrocarbons synthesized from pyrrolizidine alkaloid compounds that he took up as a caterpillar, bound together in a lipid base. If she is willing, he touches her with his hair pencils, painting her antennae with more of his pheromone bouquet, and copulation soon follows.

▲ *Ithomia arduinna arduinna*, Tambopata National
Reserve, Peru (Nymphalidae: Danaiinae)
The sexes of d'Almeida's Glasswing (*Ithomia arduinna*) are essen-
tially alike. Males (left) have a raised blister on the leading edge,
or costa, of the hindwing that contains long, hair-like androconial
scales. He exposes these during courtship so that he can waft

▲ *Melitaea athalia*, Switzerland
(Nymphalidae: Nymphalinae)
Male Heath Fritillaries (*Melitaea athalia*) patrol for
females in clearings, flying close to the ground
with alternating flaps and glides. The female,
loaded down with her eggs, flies with much more
effort. After mating she will seek a suitable site
near a food plant, usually on a dead leaf or under
a bramble leaf, before laying a clutch of up to
150 eggs. She is picky about her choice, and may
avoid some species of plants even though her
larvae are able to eat them.

▶ *Heliconius cydno cydnides*, Colombia (captive)
(Nymphalidae: Heliconiinae)
Many *Heliconius* butterflies mate before the female emerges from
the chrysalis. The male White-barred Longwing (*Heliconius cydno*),
however, courts females in the usual way. In Costa Rica *H. cydno*
and the Sapho Longwing (*H. sapho*) mimic each other, but *H. sapho*
females mate in the chrysalis; the difference may prevent mating
with the wrong species. Female *Heliconius* that mate in the chrysalis
generally mate only once, but those such as *H. cydno* that mate as
mature adults may do so with several different partners.

◄ *Erebia aethiops* female (above) and male (below), Switzerland (Nymphalidae: Satyrinae)

Evolutionary chance may determine whether a male seeking a mate patrols for her on the wing or watches from a perch. Most *Erebia* butterflies live in tundra or alpine meadows, habitats without tall bushes or other good perching sites. Patrolling is probably their best mate-finding strategy. The Scotch Argus (*Erebia aethiops*) is a lowland butterfly that prefers warm, open woodlands, where perching ought to be favored. Nonetheless it continues to patrol, suggesting that its open-country ancestors may have lost the ability to switch.

◄ *Aporia crataegi*, Switzerland (Pieridae: Pierinae)

Butterfly copulation can take some time – anywhere from 15 minutes or so to (in rare cases) several days. A mating pair of Black-veined Whites (*Aporia crataegi*) may remain locked together for several hours. How long butterflies need to copulate may depend on temperature (mating takes longer on cooler days) and how long it has been since the male last mated.

◄ *Parthenos sylvia*, Vietnam (Nymphalidae: Limenitidinae)
▲ *Ypthima baldus*, Palawan, Philippines (Nymphalidae: Satyrinae)

These two Oriental pairings show Common Five-Rings (*Ypthima baldus*) (above) and a male Clipper (*Parthenos sylvia*) (left) joined to his considerably larger mate (right). Almost all male butterflies start copulation by bending their abdomen to the side to grasp the female, then rotating around until the pair face in opposite directions. Once they are coupled, he injects her with a tough-walled sac, or spermatophore, packed with sperm and other substances. It may be days or months before she digests the spermatophore and the sperm escape to fertilize her eggs.

▲ *Acraea issoria*, Cuc Phuong National Park, Vietnam (Nymphalidae: Heliconiinae)
◀ *Actinote momina*, Manu National Park, Peru (Nymphalidae: Heliconiinae)

The Yellow Coster (*Acraea issoria*) and the Peru Altinote (*Actinote momina*) belong to the Tribe Acraeini. Once a male of this tribe has finished mating, he blocks up the female's mating tube with a waxy plug, or sphragis ("seal" in Greek). The sphragis acts as a chastity belt, preventing her from mating again. A few other butterflies, including some swallowtails, do the same. In some, including apollos (*Parnassius* spp.), the sphragis is external and serves as a warning to other males that the female has already mated.

▲ *Chlosyne lacinia*, Chiripo National Park, Costa Rica
(Nymphalidae: Nymphalinae)

The Bordered Patch (*Chlosyne lacinia*) ranges from the southwestern United States to Bolivia and Peru. Males are hilltoppers, defending a patch of ground near a landmark plant where they can watch for arriving females. In *Chlosyne* spp. the female's eggs are mature when she leaves the chrysalis, and their weight is so great that she can barely fly. After mating she will lay a cluster of about 100 eggs on the underside of a leaf of a sunflower, ragweed or related plant.

Butterfly Eggs

▲ ◄ *Iphiclides podalirius*, Switzerland (Papilionidae: Papilioninae)
► *Pieris bryoniae*, Switzerland (Pieridae: Pierinae)

Butterfly eggs vary considerably in structure and shape. Swallowtails lay large, smooth-surfaced, spherical eggs. The eggs of the Scarce Swallowtail (*Iphiclides podailurus*) (top) are white at first (upper left) but become cream after a few days, deepening to pink and finally to black – actually the color of the caterpillar inside the transparent shell (upper right). Whites and sulphurs lay upright fluted eggs, often tinted orange or pink – such as those of the Mountain Green-veined White (*Pieris bryoniae*) (middle) – presumably to warn other gravid females that the spot has already been taken.

► *Papilio machaon*, Switzerland (Papilionidae: Papilioninae)

Old World Swallowtail (*Papilio machaon*) females are highly selective when picking their plants, and they will reject some that its caterpillars are quite capable of eating – only the best will do. In an evolutionary sense it may be better for egg-laying adults to focus on a narrow range of plants than to risk making a mistake. Mistakes can be costly; Scarce Swallowtails (*Iphiclides podalirius*) in Spain occasionally lay their eggs on unfamiliar introduced plants, and their young do very poorly.

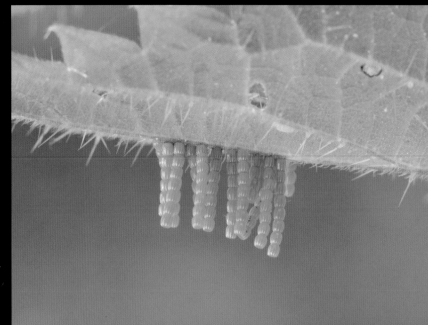

▲ *Araschnia levana*, Switzerland (Nymphalidae: Nymphalinae)

The Map (*Araschnia levana*), a widespread Eurasian butterfly, lays her eggs in long chains on the underside of nettle leaves. Maps are bivoltine – they appear in two broods per year – and the spring and summer forms look very different from one another. This is a spring-brood Map. Her eggs will eventually develop into the much darker and more contrastingly colored summer brood. Summer-brood Maps in turn produce young that overwinter as pupae, to emerge as the next year's spring Maps.

◤ *Araschnia levana*, Switzerland (Nymphalidae: Nymphalinae)

The egg chains of the Map (*Araschnia levana*) may be an adaptation to their host plant. Nettles (*Urtica* spp.) produce long clusters of tiny green flowers, and the egg chains of the Map resem-

Caterpillars

From the egg emerges the caterpillar, the stage in which many butterflies spend most of their active lives. Caterpillars are, by and large, eating machines, storing up most or all of the protein they will need as adults and taking up plant compounds that may protect them against predators throughout their lives.

As a caterpillar grows, it molts (sheds its outer cuticle) every few days or weeks, changing its appearance – sometimes drastically – as it does so. The stage between molts is called an instar, and butterfly caterpillars usually go through five of them. The fifth instar is the one that does far and away the most eating, in a final rush to take in enough food to see the caterpillar through its transformation into a pupa and, ultimately, into an adult.

A caterpillar is about as unlike an adult butterfly as a creature can be and still share the same set of genes. Its hard chewing mandibles, though composed of much the same elements as the adult's coiled proboscis, are totally unlike it in structure and function. The caterpillar lacks the adult's compound eyes and (of course) wings. It gets about instead on a combination of six real legs – far stubbier than the adult's – on its thorax and a set of soft, hook-bearing "false legs," or prolegs, that arise from the third, fourth, fifth, sixth and tenth segments of its abdomen. Its head bears spinnerets: glands whose liquid effusion, on hitting the air, turns into strands of silk. Adult butterflies may be able to fly, but only caterpillars can spin.

▲ ▲ *Papilio machaon*, Switzerland
(Papilionidae: Papilioninae)
▲ *Apatura iris*, Switzerland
(Nymphalidae: Apaturinae)
Most butterfly caterpillars, including the Old World Swallowtail (*Papilio machaon*) (top) and the Purple Emperor (*Apatura iris*) (above), are voracious leaf-eaters with massive toothed chewing mandibles and digestive tracts that take up most of their innards. Caterpillars have to process the maximum amount of chewed-up leaf in the least possible time. Their guts are basically simple tubes dominated by an immense midgut where they do most of their digesting. The faster that leaf proteins pass from the midgut into their systems, the more the caterpillars can eat.

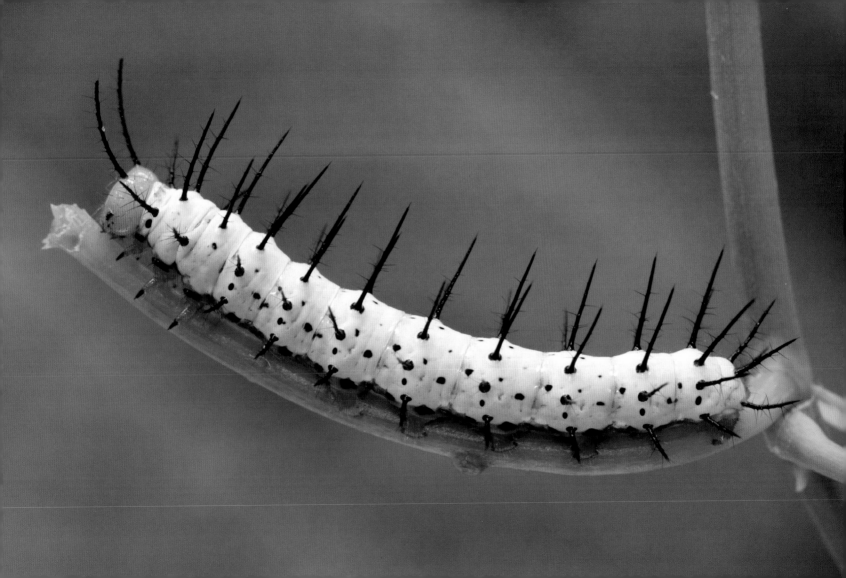

Caterpillar Variety
Swallowtails

▼ *Papilio machaon* early instar, Switzerland (Papilionidae: Papilioninae)
▲ *Papilio machaon* fourth instar, Switzerland (Papilionidae: Papilioninae)
▶ *Papilio machaon* fifth instar, Switzerland (Papilionidae: Papilioninae)

Early-instar swallowtail caterpillars are dark, tubercle-studded and quite unlike the colorful creatures most become with later molts. Old World Swallowtails (*Papilio machaon*) (left) start out looking like bird droppings, with a white saddle across the abdomen contributing to the illusion. By the fourth instar (above) the saddle has almost vanished. The fifth and final instar (right) is bright lime green, ringed with black and dotted with orange, red or yellow. This transformation from hatchling to fully grown caterpillar takes about a month.

◄ *Papilio nireus* last instar, Jozani Chwaka Bay National Park, Zanzibar, Tanzania (Papilionidae: Papilioninae)

This is probably a caterpillar of the Narrow Green-banded Swallowtail (*Papilio nireus*), a forest butterfly found throughout much of sub-Saharan Africa. It feeds on a number of host plants, including citrus trees, and molts after about four weeks into a pupa that looks like a curled-up dead leaf. What looks – and is probably meant to look, a least to predators – like a snake's eye is actually a marking on the caterpillar's thorax. Its head, with the real eyes, is far less obvious.

◄ *Iphiclides podalirius* fifth instar, Switzerland (Papilionidae: Papilioninae)

The fifth-instar caterpillar of the Scarce Swallowtail (*Iphiclides podalirius*) lacks the bold markings of many other swallowtail caterpillars. Its pattern of fine lines recalls the midrib and side veins of the leaves of sloe or plum, its usual host plants. The caterpillar spends much of the day resting on the surface of a leaf that it has covered with silk, leaving it only for feeding bouts of five minutes or so on nearby leaves.

▲ *Papilio demodocus* last instar, Madagascar
(Papilionidae: Papilioninae)

The Citrus Swallowtail (*Papilio demodocus*) is a widespread African
butterfly introduced in Madagascar, where three close relatives live
nowhere else and where its ancestors may have evolved. For the
first four instars, its caterpillars resemble bird droppings. The fifth
and final instar is usually green and blends in well on citrus trees,
its customary host plant. In some areas there is also a yellow form,
which appears to be better camouflaged on the alternative smaller-
leaved food plants the butterflies use in parts of southern Africa.

▲ *Anteos clorinde* last instar, Colombia (Pieridae: Coliadinae)
◄ *Colias alfacariensis*, Switzerland (Pieridae: Coliadinae)
The caterpillars of pierid butterflies are usually elongated, narrow-bodied and various shades of green, covered with short bristles and creased with a series of close-set ringlike folds. The caterpillars of Berger's Clouded Yellow (*Colias alfacariensis*) are typical of the family. The White Angled-Sulphur (*Anteos clorinde*) is a tropical American species that ranges from the southwestern United States to Paraguay. Its caterpillars feed on senna (*Cassia spectabilis*); they are green if they eat its leaves but yellow if they feed on its flowers.

Brush-footed Butterflies

▶ *Danaus plexippus* fourth instar, Colombia (captive) (Nymphalidae: Danaiinae)

Monarch larvae (*Danaus plexippus*) are the best-known butterfly caterpillars in North America. The pattern of yellow, black and white bands on this fourth-instar caterpillar, surmounted by two sets of whip-like filaments, resembles that of related butterflies. Some, such as the Queen (*D. gilippus*) and the African Monarch or Plain Tiger (*D. chrysippus*), add a third set of whips. The pattern serves as a warning that these caterpillars are laced with cardiac glycosides that they take up from their milkweed hosts, and thus are to be avoided.

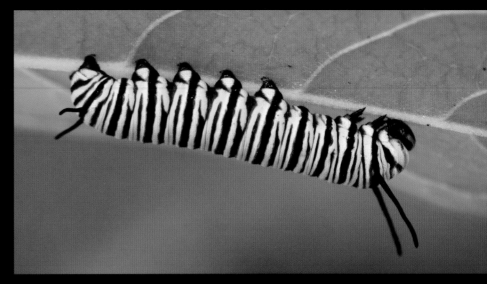

▶ *Tithorea harmonia* last instar, Manu National Park, Peru (Nymphalidae: Danaiinae)

Ithomiine butterflies are famously unpalatable but, unlike other milkweed butterflies, most get their toxins from the flowers they visit as adults. The Harmonia Tiger (*Tithorea harmonia*), a "primitive" ithomiine, is an exception. Its black-and-white-banded caterpillar, crowned with paired whip-like filaments, recalls the warningly colored larva of its distant cousin the Monarch. As with Monarchs, it is the caterpillar that loads up with toxins, in this case pyrrolizidine alkaloids from its host plant, the vine *Prestonia acutifolia* (Apocynaceae).

▶ *Mechanitis polymnia* last instar, Colombia (captive) (Nymphalidae: Danaiinae)

The Orange-spotted Tiger Clearwing (*Mechanitis polymnia*), an "advanced" ithomiine, lays clutches of 10 to 40 eggs on *Solanum* spp. and related plants. Its caterpillars are not warningly colored, carry no alkaloids, and are at risk from predatory ants. They have a unique way of hiding: their skin, or cuticle, contains lipids that resemble those produced by their host plants. These lipids serve as a sort of chemical camouflage; the ants don't seem to realize they are there and will even crawl over them without attacking.

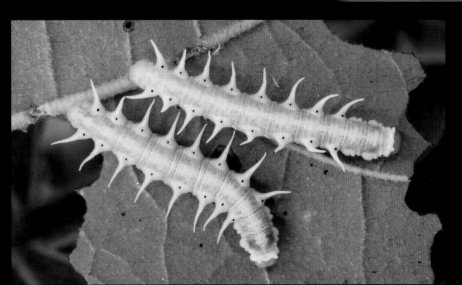

▲ *Caligo telamonius* second instar, Colombia (captive) (Nymphalidae: Satyrinae)

Owl butterfly caterpillars feed on the leaves of bananas, ginger and *Heliconia*. They spend the day anchored to a silken mat spun on the surface of a leaf or, as they grow older, a stalk, sallying forth to feed at dusk or by night. Young caterpillars, such as these second-in-star Pale Owl Butterfly (*Caligo telamonius*) larvae, rest and feed in closely packed groups. The fifth-instar caterpillar frequently rests alone, on the trunk of its food plant or on another plant nearby.

◄ *Morpho telemachus* last instar, Manu National Park Peru (Nymphalidae: Satyrinae)

Like owl butterflies, broods of some morpho caterpillars, including *Morpho telemachus*, spend the day grouped together on a silken mat spun on a leaf or, in later stages, a branch or trunk. Before pupating they may mass in groups of several hundred. Other *Morpho* species are solitary. Morphos can be slow developers; the larva of the White Morpho (*Morpho polyphemus*), a butterfly that lives in cool mountain cloud forests and feeds on particularly nonnutritious plants, takes 10 months to reach full growth.

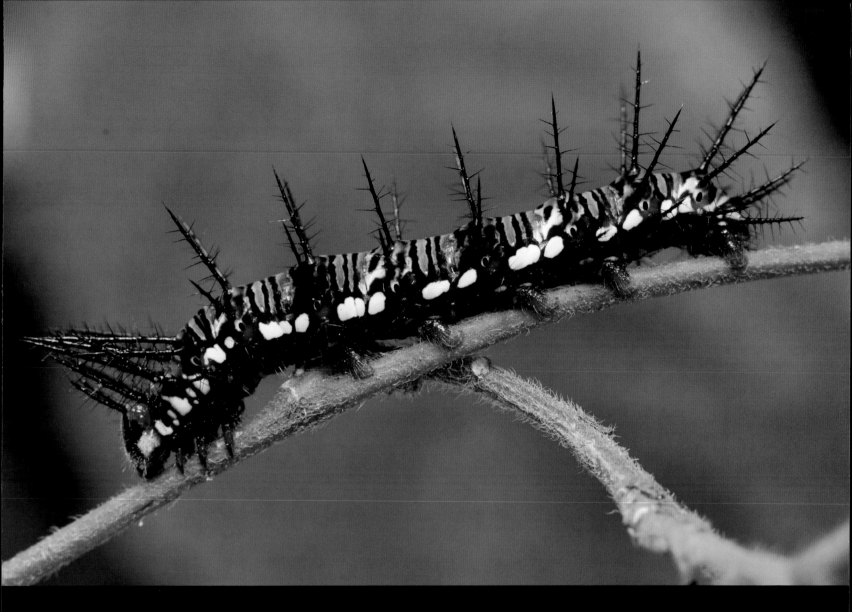

▲ *Dryas iulia* last instar, Colombia (captive)
(Nymphalidae: Heliconiinae)

The caterpillar of the Julia Longwing (*Dryas iulia*) is decorated with a
bizarre series of branched, easily broken spines. It feeds on passion
vines (*Passiflora* spp.). Julia eggs hatch after four or five days and
the caterpillars can complete their growth in less than three weeks.
Young caterpillars build shelters by partially cutting away a portion
of a leaf and waiting for it to wither. They retreat to these resting sites when threatened; their shelters appear to protect them
against predatory ants.

▲ *Siproeta epaphus* fifth instar, Colombia (captive) (Nymphalidae: Heliconiinae)
◄ *Siproeta stelenes* penultimate instar, Colombia (captive) (Nymphalidae: Heliconiinae)

Mature caterpillars of the Malachite (*Siproeta stelenes*) and the Rusty-tipped Page (*S. epaphus*) boast a fearsome-looking array of brightly colored spines. Their armament should be enough to make predators think twice. Some scientists have reported that rubbing the spines on one's hand produces an irritating itchy rash that lasts for several hours, but others have handled them without problems. Whether the caterpillars are unpalatable may depend on their host plants (Acanthaceae), some of which contain toxins while others do not.

▶ *Hamadryas feronia*
last instar, Colombia
(captive) (Nymphalidae:
Biblidinae)

Late-instar *Hamadryas* caterpillars such as this Variable
Cracker (*Hamadryas feronia*)
spend much of their time sitting
humped and motionless. If
disturbed, they strike out with
the spiky horns behind their
heads. In some species several
caterpillars forage together
on the same leaf. As they grow
older, fewer are found together,
partly because they wriggle
violently when disturbed and
may knock one another off the
leaf. Cracker caterpillars are
frequently attacked by parasitic
flies (Tachinidae), whose larvae
devour their hosts from the
inside.

▲ *Apatura iris* fall instar, Switzerland (Nymphalidae: Apaturinae)
◣ *Apatura iris*, Switzerland (Nymphalidae: Apaturinae)
The caterpillar of the Purple Emperor (*Apatura iris*) spends much of its early life rest-
ing on a silken pad on the midrib of a willow leaf, facing the leaf's base. As it grows

◄ *Aglais urticae*, Aargau Jura Park, Switzerland (Nymphalidae: Nymphalinae)
◣ *Aglais [Inachis] io*, Switzerland (Nymphalidae: Nymphalinae)
▼ *Araschnia levana*, Switzerland (Nymphalidae: Nymphalinae)

The caterpillars of the Map (*Araschnia levana*), Peacock (*Aglais io*) and Small Tortoiseshell (*Aglais urticae*), three common European brush-footed butterflies, feed on stinging nettles (*Urtica* spp.). They are close relatives, and their common ancestor probably fed on nettles too. All three are communal, feeding in groups until they are nearly mature. Peacock and Tortoiseshell caterpillars spin silken tents that the brood uses for shelter. They bask in groups, and their daytime body temperature is often higher than that of close but solitary relatives.

▲ *Melitaea phoebe*, Switzerland
(Nymphalidae: Nymphalinae)
▶ *Melitaea didyma*, Switzerland
(Nymphalidae: Nymphalinae)

Knapweed (*Melitaea phoebe*) and Spotted (*Melitaea didyma*)
Fritillaries may have two or three broods a year. In early life
the broods are communal, living and feeding together in
silken webs, but the caterpillars disperse as they grow older.
Early-instar caterpillars from the final brood of the season
hibernate together in nests, or hibernacula, that are spe-
cially woven for the purpose. Spotted Fritillary caterpillars
often use dead leaves or flower heads as a superstructure for
their winter nests.

▲ *Hypolycaena erylus teatus*, Koh Samui, Thailand (Lycaenidae: Theclinae)

The caterpillars of more than half of all lycaenid butterflies, and about one-third of metalmarks, associate with ants. Many cannot survive without them. In tropical Asia, female Common Tits (*Hypolycaena erylus*) looking for a place to lay their eggs seek out colonies of highly aggressive Weaver Ants (*Oecophylla smaragdina*). The ants attend to the caterpillars constantly, and in return the caterpillars supply the ants with a nutritious liquid. Caterpillars of the Ciliate Blue (*Anthene emolus*) spend their lives in the Weaver Ants' woven-leaf nest and will not feed outside it.

Caterpillar Defenses

Caterpillars have a number of ways of defending themselves. Some are disguised as twiglets, bird droppings or other unpalatable objects. They may use their own droppings, or frass, as a disguise or a shelter, or they may eject them as far from their host plant as possible to avoid leaving clues for ants and other predators. Many feed by night and hide in a shelter by day. Skipper caterpillars build shelters from cut and folded leaves held together with silk. If all else fails, a besieged caterpillar can escape on a silken line, or simply drop from its host plant into the leaf litter.

Larger caterpillars, and those that load their bodies with toxic substances from their food plants, may try to look as conspicuous and threatening as possible, especially in the later instars after they have built up their chemical defenses. Warning, or aposematic, color patterns alert predators that the caterpillar bearing them is one to avoid. Threatening behavior can be especially startling from a caterpillar that up till then was blending into its background. Butterfly caterpillar threats are usually a bluff. A few nymphalid caterpillars have spines that release chemicals capable of repelling ants, and some have been reported to cause rashes on human skin, but none have the fearsomely venomous bristles of some moth caterpillars.

◥ *Anthocharis cardamines,* Switzerland (Pieridae: Pierinae)
▶ *Colias alfacariensis* early instar, Switzerland (Pieridae: Coliadinae)
Smaller caterpillars, or larger ones in their early instars, usually rely on camouflage. Pierid caterpillars such as Orange-tips (*Anthocharis cardamines*) (top) can blend imperceptibly into the background, and a young Berger's Clouded Yellow (*Colias alfacariensis*) (right) may be almost invisible among the flowers of Horseshoe Vetch (*Hippocrepis comosa*). In addition, some pierids have fluid-secreting hairs that repel ants, and many tropical pierid caterpillars are known to be unpalatable to birds.

◀ *Heraclides thoas*, Colombia (captive) (Papilionidae: Papilioninae)

Swallowtail caterpillars have a unique defense: a bright orange forked gland, the osmeterium, which is usually kept tucked away behind the head. When a startled caterpillar, such as this Thoas Swallowtail (*Heraclides thoas*), snaps its osmeterium into view, the gland releases an odoriferous chemical cocktail. The osmeterium of an early-instar Eastern Tiger Swallowtail (*Papilio glaucus*) secretes some 50 terpene compounds that repel ants. Like other swallowtails, the caterpillar switches as it matures to acid defenses that may discourage larger predators such as lizards – but not, apparently, birds.

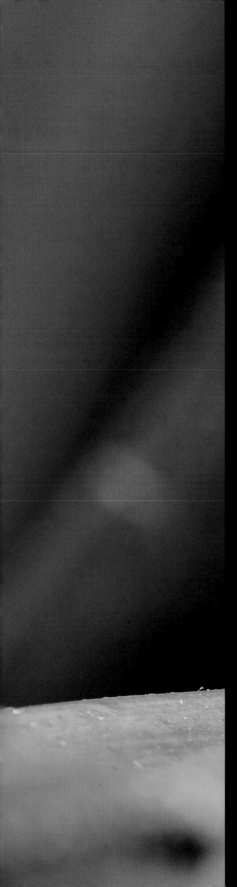

◀ *Papilio* sp. fifth instar, Cameron Highlands, West Malaysia (Papilionidae: Papilioninae)

Many swallowtail caterpillars, such as this one from Malaysia, seem to stare at the observer with a pair of snakelike eyespots. The caterpillar can heighten the effect by inflating the segments behind its head, bringing its false eyes into even greater prominence. Even caterpillars without eyespots can do this. Experiments have shown that both eyespots and an inflated front end will put off hungry birds; oddly, using both does not seem to provide more protection than using one or the other.

▲ *Morpho telemachus*, Manu National Park, Peru (Nymphalidae: Satyrinae)

Morpho caterpillars, including this *Morpho telemachus*, emit an odor like rotten tomatoes and secrete a liquid that they work through their body hairs. Neither secretion seems to be irritating. If touched, the caterpillar will rear up and flick its head from side to side, as though trying to impale its attacker on its bristles, but the bristles seem to be harmless. It may be bluffing, imitating the caterpillars of some moths whose bristles can cause serious pain and even death.

Metamorphosis

Butterflies and moths, like flies, beetles, bees and wasps, are holometabolous, meaning that they pass through four distinct stages of life: egg, larva, pupa and adult, or imago. Their growth and transformation are under the control of two classes of hormones. Ecdysteroids stimulate a caterpillar to molt. Juvenoids cause it to develop into larger and larger instars – but the hormones must be absent at a critical stage for the caterpillar to change into a pupa and eventually an adult.

The pupal stage is necessary. So completely different is the caterpillar from the adult that for the one to transform into the other, its entire body must shut down. The crawling, chewing, sexually inert larva must transform into a winged nectar-sipping creature whose prime functions are mating, breeding and flight. Inside the seemingly quiescent pupa, much of the larval body disappears entirely. Cells that have lain undifferentiated grow into the new structures of the adult; new muscles grow, and the nervous system rewires itself to operate them. The process may take days, weeks or, in species that hiber-

▲◥ ▶◢ *Papilio machaon*, Switzerland
(Papilionidae: Papilioninae)
An Old World Swallowtail (*Papilio machaon*)
caterpillar about to pupate spins a button of silk
that the pupa grips with a hooked anal append-
age, called a cremaster, and adds a silken girdle
around its waist for support. That done, it sheds
and discards its final larval cuticle, revealing the
pupa beneath. In the cooler parts of its range,
it winters as a pupa and emerges the following
spring. In warmer areas, caterpillars hatched in
spring pupate and emerge in a single year; it is
their offspring that hibernate.

◄ *Papilio machaon,*
Switzerland (Papilionidae:
Papilioninae)

A pupa's chief defense is concealment. Old World Swallowtail
(*Papilio machaon*) pupae are normally brown in autumn, the better
to blend with the dying foliage. In
many butterflies the pupa can be
either green or brown, depending
on the color and texture of the
background and the temperature
and day length (a sign of approaching winter) that the caterpillar
experiences before it molts. In swallowtails, release of a "browning"
hormone results in a brown pupa
instead of a green one; in other butterfly families different hormones
are involved.

▲ ◤ ▶ *Apatura iris*, Switzerland (Nymphalidae: Apaturinae)

In June, after living as a caterpillar for almost a year, including a winter spent in hibernation, the Purple Emperor (*Apatura iris*) suspends itself by its hooked cremaster from a silken button on the underside of a willow leaf and molts into a well-camouflaged chrysalis. Its cuticle, soft at first, soon hardens into a tough protective shell. Like other nymphalid caterpillars (but unlike swallowtails and pierids), it does not support itself with a silken girdle. It will emerge about two weeks later as an adult butterfly.

◄ *Gonepteryx rhamni*, Switzerland (Pieridae: Coliadinae)
▼ *Phoebis sennae*, Colombia (captive) (Pieridae: Coliadinae)

The pupae of pierids, like those of swallowtails, support themselves with a silken girdle. The outline of a Brimstone (*Gonepteryx rhamni*) pupa (left) reveals the space allotted for the developing wing. The wing itself is visible beneath the cuticle in a nearly mature chrysalis of a Cloudless Sulphur (*Phoebis sennae*) (below). Not all butterflies suspend their pupae from a leaf or stem; gossamer-wings, metalmarks and skippers lack a cremaster, and either bind themselves to a plant with silk or pupate on the ground.

▲ ▶ *Mechanitis polymnia*, Colombia (captive) (Nymphalidae: Danaiinae)
Most butterflies (except for skippers) do not enclose their pupae in a cocoon. The elegant word "chrysalis" comes, by way of Latin, from the Greek *khrusos*, or "gold" – an appropriate name for the glittering pupa of the Orange-spotted Tiger Clearwing (*Mechanitis polymnia*) of tropical America. These are being raised on a butterfly farm in Cali, Colombia. Though *Mechanitis* caterpillars often pupate together, in nature a cluster of chrysalides could attract a predator, and caterpillars may wander some distance from their host plant before pupating alone.

▸▲ ◂ ▸ *Gonepteryx rhamni*, Switzerland
(Pieridae: Coliadinae)

The emergence of a Brimstone (*Gonepteryx rhamni*) like that of other butterflies, is controlled by a hormone and triggered by environmental factors such as temperature and light. The timing is critical. Before its wings expand and harden, the adult is helpless. Most butterflies emerge at dawn, reducing their chance of being noticed. If competition for mates is high, especially for females that mate only once, males may emerge first to get a head start on their rivals. Early male emergence is called protandry.

CHAPTER 9

What Butterflies Eat

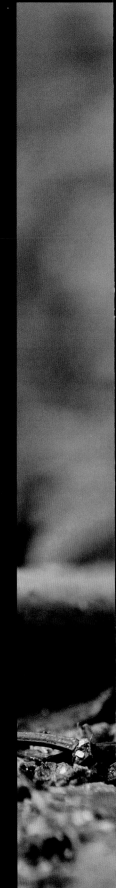

The adult butterfly emerges from its pupal skin with its feeding apparatus entirely changed from the leaf-chomping jaws of caterpillarhood. Its chewing mandibles are now reduced and useless. Instead, maxillary structures called galeae, one from each side, lock together into a long, tightly coiled tube – the proboscis, or "tongue". The proboscis acts like a combination sponge and drinking straw, drawing in liquid by capillary attraction and using a pump in the butterfly's head to create a pressure gradient that sucks the fluid into its body.

In most butterflies the proboscis extends to no more than 80% of body length, and frequently less, but in the tropical American metalmark genus *Eurybia* it is twice as long as the butterfly itself. The longest butterfly proboscis measured, at 52.7 mm (2.1 in), belonged to a skipper from Panama, the Immaculate Ruby-Eye (*Damas immaculata*).

Nectar-feeding butterflies rely largely on sight to find food. Fruit-feeding butterflies such as morphos are drawn by smell rather than sight, picking up odors with sense organs on their antennae,

mouthparts and legs. Most fruit-feeders have a modified proboscis adapted to sweeping fluid from moist surfaces. However, *Charaxes* and its relatives have a thick, strong proboscis able to pierce the skins of decaying fruits and animal carcasses.

Butterflies can be voracious feeders. A Painted Lady (*Vanessa cardui*) may visit 150 flowers in less than an hour. A Blue Morpho (*Morpho peleides*) on a rotting banana can consume more than 23% of its body weight in juices within two minutes, and almost 44% in 10 minutes.

▶ *Euphaedra hewitsoni,* Republic of the Congo (Nymphalidae: Limenitidinae)
Hewitson's Pink Forester (*Euphaedra hewitsoni*) belongs to a genus of nearly 200 gorgeous African butterflies related to admirals (Limenitidinae). Foresters search avidly for fallen fruits, especially figs, and appear to do particularly well on them. Fruit can supply nitrogen-rich nutrients that flower nectar lacks. The extra nourishment may help foresters live longer as adults – up to 10 months. Ugandan foresters fed mashed bananas produced almost twice as many eggs as those fed a sugar solution alone.

◄ *Papilio machaon*, Switzerland (Papilionidae: Papilioninae)

This newly emerged Old World Swallowtail (*Papilio machaon*), the same individual seen leaving its cocoon in the previous chapter, may be uncoiling its proboscis for the first time. The proboscis works by hydraulics, uncoiling as the butterfly pumps hemolymph – the insect version of blood – into the galeae. It is through the proboscis that the adult takes up its liquid food from flowers, fruits, wet soil or wherever else the sugars and minerals it needs to survive can be found.

◄ *Pachliopta aristolochiae*, Erawan National Park, Thailand (Papilionidae: Papilioninae)

When a Common Rose (*Pachliopta aristolochiae*) uncoils its proboscis, sensory hairs on its outer surface help the butterfly place it properly in the depths of a flower. Other sensors respond to the presence of sugars and may sense the passage of liquids up the feeding tube. If the butterfly feeds on rotting fruit, sensors detect the presence of ethanol. Sensors on other parts of its body pick up airborne compounds, and may have drawn it to the fruit in the first place.

In a Swiss Meadow

◥ *Papilio machaon*, Switzerland (Papilionidae: Papilioninae)

A summer meadow in Switzerland, filled with nectar-rich wildflowers, can be a mecca for Old World Swallowtails (*Papilio machaon*) and other butterflies. Meadow flowers tend to be broad and open, their nectar supplies available to even the shortest-tongued species. Flower-feeding butterflies drink nectar to gain energy, but they must spend energy to collect it. A flower-filled meadow not only provides a ready supply of nectar but also lowers the time and the energy a butterfly needs to fly from one flower to the next.

▶ *Lycaena virgaureae*, Switzerland (Lycaenidae: Lycaeninae)

Butterflies see flower colors, including colors in the ultra-violet range that we cannot see. They have color prefer-ences too, but color is not the only thing that draws them to a flower. Coppers such as this Scarce Copper (*Lycaena virgaureae*) prefer members of the daisy family (Asteraceae). A study of two American coppers, the Blue Copper (*L. heteronea*) and the Ruddy Copper (*L. rubidus*), in meadows in Colorado found that each species preferred different flow-ers, possibly to avoid competing or in response to chemical differences in their nectar.

Celastrina argiolus, Switzerland (Lycaenidae: Polyommatinae)

The attraction that flowers of the daisy family have for small butterflies such as coppers and the Holly Blue or Spring Azure (*Celastrina argiolus*) is not just color, or even nectar quality. Their individual florets are very short, so the tongues of small butterflies can reach their nectar. In general, butterflies will not visit flowers with nectar that is too deep for them to reach. A daisy-filled meadow is an ideal place for blues and their relatives to feed.

Aglais urticae, Switzerland (Nymphalidae: Nymphalinae)
Thymelicus sylvestris, Switzerland (Hesperiidae: Hesperiinae)

Floral depth is not the only constraint that meadow butterflies face. Butterflies with heavy bodies, small wings and high wing-loading ratios, such as the Small Tortoiseshell (*Aglais urticae*) (middle right) and the Small Skipper (*Thymelicus sylvestris*) (bottom right), are more likely to visit areas of the meadow where flowers mass together, or to concentrate on plants with multiple flowers, to reduce the energy cost of flight from flower to flower. Solitary plants with few flowers, even those with a good nectar supply, may be too costly to visit.

▲ *Argynnis paphia* - Switzerland (Nymphalidae: Heliconiinae)

Thistle flowers, with their copious supplies of nectar, draw Silver-washed Fritillaries (*Argynnis paphia*) to the meadow. This is normally a butterfly of oak and beech woodland that roosts in the treetops and feeds at bramble flowers at the forest edge in the warmer part of the day. Thistles, though, remain crucial to butter-flies, and the loss of thistle nectar as meadows are converted to farmland, plantations and housing developments is a likely factor in the recent decline of many European butterfly populations.

▲ ▲ *Gonepteryx rhamni*, Switzerland (Pieridae: Coliadinae)

▲ *Euphydryas intermedia wolfensbergeri*, Switzerland (Nymphalidae: Nymphalinae)

Unless it is probing a deep flower, a feeding butterfly's proboscis usually bends downward about a third of the way along its length. Its two sides are not hermetically sealed, and bending may allow the butterfly some control over its drinking rate. This natural kink makes it easier for its owner to probe a shallow flower while perching. A Brimstone (*Gonepteryx rhamni*) (top) or an Asian Fritillary (*Euphydryas intermedia*) (above) alighting on a thistle simply has to swivel

Butterflies, Flowers,
Fruit, Sap and Dung

Most tropical forest butterflies fall into two major ecological categories. Some – mostly swallowtails, whites
and gossamer-wings – visit flowers and feed on nectar,
while others – mostly nymphalids – feed instead on
fallen fruit or tree sap. In the depths of a tropical forest,
where flowers may be scarce at some times of year,
rotting fruit may be the best available food source. It
supplies sugars, amino acids, lipids and other nutrients
crucial to long life and high fecundity. Squinting Bush

▲ *Papilio nireus*, Africa (captive) (Papilionidae: Papioninae)

Swallowtails too are almost entirely nectar-feeders. This Narrow Green-banded Swallowtail (*Papilio nireus*), a common African species, is visiting the flowers of a tropical milkweed, *Asclepias curassavica*.

◥ *Jamides* sp., Tenom, Sabah, Malaysia (Lycaenidae: Polyommatinae)

▶ *Idea leuconoe*, Malaysia (Nymphalidae: Danaiinae)

Tropical Asian forest butterflies also divide into nectar-feeders and fruit-and-dung-feeders. Gossamer-wings, including this Caerulean (*Jamides* sp.) (top right) dwarfed by a flowering ginger (*Etlingera flavofimbriata*), are nectar-feeders. The Siam Tree Nymph (*Idea leuconoe*) (right), a nymphalid, flies in the forest canopy, where flowers are more likely to be in bloom, and relies on sight to find them. It is particularly attracted to red. Many other Asian nymphalids avoid flowers and are rarely seen away from the forest interior.

▲ *Vanessa atalanta*, Switzerland
(Nymphalidae: Nymphalinae)

Red Admirals (*Vanessa atalanta*) are flower-
feeders in summer but live well into the autumn,
when most flowers have finished blooming and
fermenting apples lie on the ground. When they
emerge in early spring they feed heavily on tree
sap, which may be the only food available. Their
Asian relative the Indian Red Admiral (*V. indica*)
can find food by sight and smell; it is known to be
attracted by the mixture of ethanol and vinegar
that tree sap and rotting fruits emit.

▲ *Dynamine postverta*, Iguaçu National Park, Brazil
(Nymphalidae: Biblidinae)

Sap and other secretions oozing from scarred trunks or broken
branches provide food sources for both tropical and temperate brush-footed butterflies, including this Four-spotted Sailor
(*Dynamine postverta*). One study in Colombia found 61 species of
nymphalid butterflies, from 35 genera and six subfamilies, feeding
on bark secretions from only seven species of tree. Bark secretions,
especially if they are infected with yeasts and other fungi, can supply sugars, alcohols and other compounds. Butterflies can literally
get drunk feeding from them.

▲ ▲ *Paralaxita damajanti,* Danum Valley Conservation Area, Sabah, Malaysia (Riodinidae: Nemeobiinae)

▲ *Diaethra clymena,* Manu National Park, Peru (Nymphalidae: Biblidinae)

Plants sometimes produce nectar from glands called extrafloral nectaries, on stems, leaves and leafstalks. Many insects, particularly ants, take advantage of them. Tropical butterflies that associate with ants, including lycaenids and metalmarks, visit extrafloral nectaries too, but other butterflies do so only occasionally. This Malay Red Harlequin (*Paralaxita damajanti*) (top) is a metalmark but is not tended by ants. Perhaps it is drinking water from the leaf's surface. The same may be true for this Widespread Eighty-eight (*Diaethria clymena*) (above), a nymphalid.

Puddling

◄ *Caleta roxus, Leptotes plinius* (Lycaenidae);
Cepora nerissa dapha, Gandaca harina,
Catopsila scylla, Eurema hecabe (Pieridae);
Graphium sp. (Papilionidae), Kheaun Sri
Nakarin National Park, Thailand

The need for mineral salts to load their spermatophores
with nuptial "gifts" draws many male butterflies, even
nectar-feeders, to the ground, a behavior called puddling.
Lycaenids, pierids and swallowtails get most of their sugar
from flowers, but the males often gather to drink from
damp soil. Assembled here in Thailand are (left to right) a
Straight Pierrot (*Caleta roxus*), a Zebra Blue (*Leptotes plinius*),
several Common Gills (*Cepora nerissa dapha*), a Tree Yellow
(*Gandaca harina*), a Jay (*Graphium* sp.), an Orange Emigrant
(*Catopsila scylla*) and a Common Grass Yellow (*Eurema
hecabe*).

◄ *Pterourus warscewiczii*, Manu National Park, Peru (Papilionidae: Papilioninae)
◣ *Graphium sarpedon*, Gunung Leuser National Park, Sumatra, Indonesia (Papilionidae: Papilioninae)
▼ *Papilio demodocus*, Jozani Chwaka Bay National Park, Zanzibar, Tanzania (Papilionidae: Papilioninae)
Swallowtails are regular puddlers, often in large, closely packed groups. Drinking here are a Cloud-frosted Swallowtail (*Pterourus warscewiczii*) (left) from tropical America, a Common Bluebottle (*Graphium sarpedon*) (bottom left) from tropical Asia and a Citrus Swallowtail (*Papilio demodocus*) (bottom right) from Africa.

► *Lamproptera curius*, Kheaun Sri Nakarin National Park, Thailand (Papilionidae: Papilioninae)
▼ *Eurytides orabilis*, Anchicaya, Colombia (Papilionidae: Papilioninae)

Desert butterflies may need water, but when rainforest butterflies puddle they are more likely topping up their sodium reserves. Here, a White Dragontail (*Lamproptera curius*) (right) and a Thick-edged Kite-Swallowtail (*Eurytides orabilis*) (below) expel jets of waste water even as they continue to drink. *Gluphisia septentrionis*, a moth, expels larger amounts of water while puddling if the sodium solution given to it is dilute. The moth is after sodium, not water, and will puddle until it has accumulated enough of it. These butterflies are probably doing the same thing.

► *Pyrrhopyge charybdis charybdis*, Iguaçu National Park, Brazil (Hesperiidae: Pyrginae)

The Charybdis Firetip (*Pyrrhopyge charybdis charybdis*) – its Spanish name means "little devil" – is a colorful tropical American skipper. Male firetips, like other male skippers, are known puddlers. They need the sodium; though male European Skippers (*Thymelicus lineola*) emerge with two to three times the sodium level of females, 32% of that goes to the female at first mating. Replenishing his sodium supply is critical to both a male's breeding success and that of his mate, who needs large amounts of sodium to produce her eggs.

▲ *Diaethria marchalii,* Risaralda, Colombia (Nymphalidae: Biblidinae)
◀ *Paulogramma pygas,* Iguaçu National Park, Brazil (Nymphalidae: Biblidinae)
↘ *Paulogramma eunomia,* Rurrenabaque, Bolivia (Nymphalidae: Biblidinae)
▶ Mixed '88's, Peru (Nymphalidae: Biblidinae)

The charming and colorful "eighty-eight" butterflies (Biblidinae) of the New World tropics are inveterate puddlers, descending after a morning spent high in the forest canopy to drink from soil, stones, road surfaces, walls or even human skin. Shown here are some of the many species: a *Diaethria marchalii*; a Godart's Numberwing or Pygas Eighty-eight (*Paulogramma pygas*); a Eunomia Numberwing or Eunomia Eighty-eight (*P. eunomia*); and (right) a group of Humboldt's Perisamas with one *D. marchalii* (and some skippers in the background).

▲ *Charaxes bernardus*, Gunung Leuser National Park,
Sumatra, Indonesia (Nymphalidae: Charaxinae)
Some male butterflies puddle but keep their sodium for their own
use. Male *Charaxes* are vigorous puddlers, but most species studied
in the Kibale Forest, Uganda, added little sodium to their spermatophores. Instead they may use the extra sodium in their unusually

◄ *Erebia pronoe*, Switzerland (Nymphalidae: Satyrinae)
Puddling is best known in tropical butterflies, but temperate butterflies, including skippers and swallowtails, can be puddlers too. The Water Ringlet (*Erebia pronoe*), a nymphalid, is confined to mountainous regions in Europe. Notice how this male is using the tip of his proboscis to sweep water from the rock he is perched on.

▼ *Chorinea sylphina*, Manu National Park, Peru (Riodinidae: Riodininae)
Puddling is not widespread among metalmarks. Only 25 out of 441 metalmark species in Ecuador have been reported to engage in it. Those that do puddle, including the Sylphina Angel (*Chorinea sylphina*), tend to have a smaller relative wing area than nonpuddlers and to be fast, erratic and agile in flight. They may need higher levels of sodium than their relatives, both to supply their flight muscles and, as almost all puddlers are males, to provide their females with copulatory gifts.

Swarms of
Butterflies

▶ **Puddling butterflies, Manu National Park, Peru**
A mass of puddling butterflies is a spectacular sight. Clouds of butterflies, often of many species, gather in the forests of tropical America, Africa and Southeast Asia and alight on a dirt road or on the damp sand beside a forest stream. Some, including this group of mostly nymphalid butterflies in Manu National Park, Peru, tend to scatter, each butterfly avoiding its neighbor. At Manu, puddlers tend to be butterflies of edges, light gaps and the canopy rather than the forest interior.

▲ ▲ *Eurytides* spp. and others, Manu National Park, Peru
(Papilionidae: Papilioninae)
▲ Mixed Pieridae, Iguazu National Park, Argentina
▶ Pieridae, Iguaçu National Park, Brazil
Puddling swallowtails and, particularly, whites and sulphurs may crowd
together in tight masses, with butterflies from other families scattered loosely
around them. Being in a large, tightly packed mass may provide safety.
Butterflies on the ground are vulnerable, and birds may be drawn to puddling
groups for an easy meal. The chance of any individual butterfly surviving an
attack seems to be greater if it is part of a confusing mass of others.

▲ Mixed Pieridae, Venezuela
▼ Pieridae, Tingo Maria, Peru

When butterflies puddle on damp soil, pierids often outnumber the rest. Nymphalids, by contrast, are more attracted to carrion and dung. Both soil and dung supply sodium, but in different concentrations. Experiments in Colorado showed that one pierid, the Green-veined White (*Pieris napi*), preferred sodium concentrations in soil to those in dung. Differences in sodium concentration may drive butterfly families to puddle on different surfaces, and may explain why the clouds of pierids that puddle on damp soil leave dung largely alone.

▲▲ *Appias nero*, Gunung Leuser National Park, Sumatra, Indonesia (Pieridae: Pierinae)
▲ *Appias sylvia* and others, Gabon (Pieridae: Pierinae)

Mixed groups of pierid butterflies in Africa and tropical Asia may center around albatrosses – not the giant seabirds, but whites in the genus *Appias*. *Appias* is primarily an Asian and Australasian genus, and one of its most colorful members, the Orange Albatross (*A. nero*), is common in tropical Asia. There are two species in the Americas and six in Africa. In the forefront of this group from Gabon is a Woodland Albatross White (*A. sylvia*), with other species of pierid behind it.

▲ *Lamproptera meges*, Cuc Phuong National Park, Vietnam (Papilionidae: Papilioninae)
◄ ▶ *Actinote momina*, Manu National Park, Peru (Nymphalidae: Heliconiinae)

In the tropics mixed swarms are the norm, but sometimes masses of a single species may puddle together. Male Green Dragontails (*Lamproptera meges*) frequently associate along the banks of Southeast Asian rivers, while in South America groups of Peru Altinotes (*Actinote momina*) stand out sharply against the gray rocks of a streambed. Altinotes are unpalatable and warningly colored; massing In a group may reinforce the impact of their warning.

Butterflies in Their Environment

Aside from the oceans and the Antarctic, butterflies are everywhere. They have adapted to almost every terrestrial habitat on earth, from tropical rainforest to deserts and arctic tundra. They have evaded a host of predators by using concealment and bluff, and they have met the challenges of hostile environments with solutions ranging from built-in antifreeze to the greatest mass migration on the planet.

▲ *Parnassius apollo*, Switzerland (Papilionidae: Parnassiinae)
▶ *Caligo atreus*, La Selva, Costa Rica (Nymphalidae: Satyrinae)
An Apollo (Parnassius apollo) seeking nectar in a flower-filled temperate meadow in the Swiss Alps, and a Yellow-edged Giant Owl (Caligo atreus) clinging to the trunk of a tropical rainforest tree in Costa Rica, exemplify the great range of habitats and lifestyles butterflies have adopted.

Predators and Parasites

Butterflies and their eggs, caterpillars and pupae are eaten by ants, mantids, dragonflies, spiders, frogs, toads, lizards, birds, mice, bats, monkeys and, presumably, anything else that can catch them. They, in their turn, have developed defenses against this onslaught. Pressure from predators and parasites has driven much of butterfly evolution, including some of the most superb and exact examples of camouflage and mimicry in the animal kingdom.

Butterflies have probably been providing meals for birds since the two groups first evolved. They have evolved a host of ways to escape their pursuers, from toxic or unpalatable body chemistry to warning colors and patterns, increasingly sophisticated camouflage, evasive flight maneuvers and mimicry. Birds in turn have developed ways to find and catch their prey and to discriminate among butterflies worth eating and others best avoided. The more skilled the predators have become, the more intense has been the selection pressure on prey and the more refined butterfly defenses have become.

The more sophisticated the predator, the more refined its selective force. Some birds, such as jays, tend to avoid any butterfly with warning coloration. In tropical America, though, the Rufous-tailed Jacamar (*Galbula ruficauda*) regularly attacks brightly colored butterflies, snapping them up on the wing with its extremely long, thin bill. Young jacamars learn to recognize the details of specific butterfly patterns, and older birds will attack butterflies they do not recognize to see if they are palatable. With a predator like that around, the more likely it is that imperfect mimics will be weeded out, and the greater the pressure on survivors to look as much like their models as possible.

▲ *Morpho achilles*, Tingo Maria, Peru
(Nymphalidae: Satyrinae)
A butterfly in flight can avoid a pursuing bird by declaring through its color pattern that it is unpalatable, or by taking evasive maneuvers. Palatable butterflies such as morphos, which do not rely on mimicry, have more powerful flight muscles and faster acceleration than distasteful butterflies and their mimics. Though they usually fly slowly and erratically, morphos can outfly a pursuing bird. If they fail, their dazzling iridescence may distract the attacker. Like this Banded Blue Morpho (*Morpho achilles*), they may escape with only torn wings.

Spiders and Mantids

▲ *Misumena vatia* and *Araschnia levana*, Switzerland (Nymphalidae: Nymphalinae)

Spiders, as a group, devour quantities of butterflies. Crab Spiders (*Misumena vatia*) hide within flowers or near them and wait for their prey, their bright colors blending with the petals. They primarily take bees and nectar-feeding flies but will not pass up a butterfly if it comes their way. This one has captured a Map (*Araschnia levana*).

▲ Spider with caterpillar, Madagascar

Many spiders are ambush predators. This Malagasy spider may have relied on its camouflage to take a caterpillar unawares. Some butterfly defense mechanisms, including the false "heads" on the hindwings of hairstreaks, may have evolved in response to spider attacks. When jumping spiders, which normally attack the head end of their prey, threaten Red-banded Hairstreaks (*Calycopis cecrops*), the butterflies turn their false heads toward them and wiggle their false antennae, usually convincing the spider to make a futile attack on the wrong end.

▲ *Pseudocreobotra* sp. nymph (Hymenopodidae) with pierid butterfly, Gabon

Juveniles, or nymphs, of African Spiny Flower Mantises (*Pseudocreobotra* spp.) are remarkable flower mimics, capable of changing color to match the flowers they hide on. They will sit – sometimes for days – amid a cluster of flowers, waiting for butterflies, their main prey, to investigate the blossoms. The nymphs are skilled at snatching in midair any butterfly that ventures too close. This one is devouring a captured sulphur.

▲ *Creobroter gemmatus* (Hymenopodidae) with Acraea issora, Cuc Phuong National Park, Vietnam (Nymphalidae: Heliconiinae)

In Asia, Jeweled Flower Mantises (*Creobroter gemmatus*) are skilled butterfly-catchers. This adult has captured a Yellow Coster (*Acraea issora*).

Parasitic Wasps and Flies

Some of the most devastating butterfly predators attack their victims from within. Parasitic wasps and flies lay their eggs on – or in – butterfly eggs, caterpillars or pupae, and their young literally eat their hosts from the inside out. Some parasitoids, so called because, unlike true parasites, their adults live as free-flying insects, specialize on only one or a few species of butterfly. Ichneumon wasps of the genus *Trogus*, for example, lay their eggs only on swallowtails. A single butterfly species may be host to a whole community of parasitoids. A study of the Scarce Swallowtail (*Iphiclides podailurus*) in Spain found that its eggs and larvae were victimized by six species of wasp and two flies.

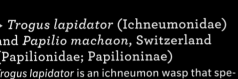 *Trogus lapidator* (Ichneumonidae) and *Papilio machaon*, Switzerland (Papilionidae; Papilioninae)

Trogus lapidator is an ichneumon wasp that specializes in parasitizing only two butterfly species, the Old World Swallowtail (*Papilio machaon*) and its close relative the Southern Swallowtail (*P. alexanor*). It is one of the most serious predators that swallowtail caterpillars face. A female wasp seeks out a caterpillar and injects it with a single egg. The caterpillar lives to pupate, but it is the wasp, not the butterfly, that emerges from the chrysalis, boring its way out through a hole in the side.

Camouflage, Masquerade and Mimicry

The best way to avoid becoming the victim of a predator is to avoid being found in the first place. For predators that rely on vision, butterflies accomplish this in two main ways: camouflage (blending into the background) and masquerade (trying to look like something else, preferably inedible). Camouflage relies on not being seen. Masquerade relies on being mistaken for something else: a twig, a leaf or a bird dropping. Studies of moths, past masters at both, suggest that both strategies fool predators, but they are not identical. Evolving toward one or the other has consequences: a caterpillar that looks like a bird dropping doesn't have to blend into its background and may be able to survive on a wider range of host plants than a camouflage artist.

▲ ▲ *Hamadryas feronia*, Colombia (captive) (Nymphalidae: Biblidinae)
▲ *Hamadryas feronia*, Morrocoy National Park, Venezuela (Nymphalidae: Biblidinae)
The Variable Cracker (*Hamadryas feronia*) depends on camouflage. Crackers perch head down on tree trunks, where they can blend in beautifully with the bark (above) if they pick the right tree. Their color changes with age (top), and these butterflies are known to prefer backgrounds that match their appearance. Males, however, sometimes perch on patches of white bark, possibly to make themselves more visible to passing females; they may be sacrificing

◀ *Anteos clorinde*, Belize (Pieridae: Coliadinae)
When perched with folded wings, the White Angled-Sulphur (*Anteos clorinde*) uses its wing shape, color and pattern to masquerade quite convincingly as a green leaf. In flight, or when perched on a flower with its wings held partly open, it is quite conspicuous. The upper wings of both sexes are white, with a yellow patch on each forewing that reflects strongly in the ultraviolet range. This reflectance may serve as a signal between the sexes; it is absent on the wings' undersurface.

◀ *Fountainea nessus* male, Manu National Park, Peru (Nymphalidae: Charaxinae)
The Superb Leafwing (*Fountainea nessus*) masquerades as a dead leaf, or perhaps the base of a broken leaf, with its tail standing in for a projecting midrib. In the heat of the day it rests quietly on leaves or branches, where it is presumably easily overlooked. As in many other leaf mimics, the male's upper side, invisible until the insect flies, is the opposite of concealing. His upperwings are black, with iridescent bright pink bands across the forewing that are overlaid with a violet sheen.

◀ *Steroma* sp., Coroico, Bolivia (Nymphalidae: Satyrinae)
The mottled satyrs (*Steroma* spp.) form a small group of five species (two still unnamed) from mountain forests in northern South America. When they perch, their forewings are tucked out of sight and their crenellated, mottled hindwings give the impression of a tuft of lichen, a clod of earth or a badly decomposed leaf. They fly slowly, close to the ground, where they are easily overlooked. Unlike the other masqueraders here, they are not concealing a colorful upper surface; aside from the mottled underside of the hindwing, they are mostly dull brown.

Tropical Asia is home to the most thoroughgoing leaf mimics in the butterfly world. Alfred Russel Wallace called the mimicry of the oakleaf butterflies (*Kallima* spp.) "the most wonderful and undoubted case of protective resemblance in a butterfly that I have ever seen." He noted that, despite their "striking and showy" upper surfaces, "adorned with a broad band of orange on a deep bluish ground," their underside is almost an exact copy of a fungus-spotted dead leaf. They are tremendously variable, just as real dead leaves are: "out of fifty specimens no two can be found exactly alike." Even the way they sit on a branch, with the tail of the wing touching the stem, adds to the resemblance. As Wallace commented, "We thus have size, colour, form, markings and habits, all combining together to produce a disguise that may be said to be absolutely perfect."

▲▲ *Melanitis* sp., India (Nymphalidae: Satyrinae)
▲ *Thaumantis klugius candika*, Gunung Leuser National Park, Sumatra, Indonesia (Nymphalidae: Satyrinae)
Asian forests contain a number of satyrine butterflies that do not masquerade as individual leaves, but they are so thoroughly camouflaged that when they land in the leaf litter, they almost disappear. The dark lines crossing the hindwings of an Evening Brown (*Melanitis* sp.) (top) and the contrasting patterns of light and dark on the Dark Blue Jungle Glory (*Thaumantis klugius candika*) (bottom) break up their outline against the scattered dead leaves, hiding them even if their shape is not particularly leaf-like

▲ *Doleschallia bisaltide*, Cuc Phuong National Park, Vietnam (Nymphalidae: Nymphalinae)
► *Kallima inacho*, Vietnam, Cat Tien National Park (Nymphalidae: Nymphalinae)

A study published in 2014 argues that the near-perfect leaf mimicry of the Orange Oakleaf (*Kallima inacho*) (right) evolved gradually, through a series of intermediate stages, from the basic nymphalid wing pattern. Each intermediate stage provided greater concealment from predators than its ancestor's. The authors were able to track many of the changes through the patterns of other living butterflies. Another Asian mimic, the Autumn Leaf (*Doleschallia bisaltide*) (above), may represent a penultimate stage – not as perfect as *Kallima*, perhaps, but still highly effective.

Mimicry

Aposematic, or warning, color patterns rely on being noticed, making a strong impression and being remembered. The learning aspect is crucial. The fewer patterns and colors a predator has to keep in mind in deciding which butterfly to avoid, the more successful the warning is likely to be. This led to the evolution of mimicry: unpalatable butterflies evolved to resemble one another (Müllerian mimicry) and palatable butterflies evolved similarities in both appearance and behavior to their unpalatable neighbors (Batesian mimicry), so that they too could benefit from the predator's learning experience.

▲ *Eresia lansdorfi*, Superagui island, Brazil (Nymphalidae: Nymphalinae)
▶ *Podotricha telesiphe*, Peru (Nymphalidae: Heliconiinae)
Both these butterflies mimic unpalatable *Heliconius* longwings. The Angle-winged Telesiphe (*Podotricha telesiphe*) (right), a highland butterfly found from Colombia to Peru, mimics the Telesiphe Longwing (*Heliconius telesiphe*). The two species fly together. In Colombia and northern Ecuador the longwing has a yellow, rather than white, band on its hindwing, and so do the Telesiphes that fly with it. Lansdorf's

Tiger Mimics

▲ *Mechanitis menapis occasiva*, Peru (Nymphalidae: Danaiinae)
Dozens of tropical American butterflies share similar black, orange and yellow wing
patterns. "Tiger mimic" complexes center around butterflies in the tribe Ithomiini.
Ithomiines can be loaded with toxic compounds, taken up as larvae from host plants
in the nightshade family (Solanaceae) or, as adults, from the alkaloid-rich nectars of
their preferred flowers. Members of the abundant and widespread genus *Mechanitis*,
including the Variable Tigerwing (*M. menapis*), both mimic larger ithomiines and
serve as models for tiger mimics from other butterfly and moth families.

▲ *Forbestra olivencia olivencia*, Peru (Nymphalidae: Danaiinae)

The more unpalatable butterfly species that share a similar pattern, the likelier predators are to learn it and the more successful a Müllerian mimicry complex will be. The Olivencia Tigerwing (*Forbestra olivencia*), a close relative of *Mechanitis*, was one of the commoner members of a tiger mimic complex involving 13 species of ithomiines studied in eastern Ecuador. How do so many similar species live together? Part of the answer may be habitat preference, including height preferences. *Forbestra* prefers deep shade, for example, while other ithomiines are commoner in sunlit gaps.

▲ *Hypoleria ocalea ocalea*, Los Llanos, Venezuela (Nymphalidae: Danaiinae)

Hypoleria ocalea is another ithomiine tiger mimic, though it is not particularly close to *Mechanitis* and *Forbestra*. The complex interrelationships among members of different mimicry complexes may be indicators of the health of the tropical forest ecosystems where they live. A study in a Brazilian forest reserve found that mimicry rings involving clearwing butterflies whose members fed on rotting fruit, including *Hypoleria* spp., did well in the depths of intact forest, but other complexes dominated in fragmented forest outside the reserve, where there were open, sunny areas.

▲ *Mimoides xynias*, Misahualli, Ecuador (Papilionidae: Papilioninae)

Mimoides caterpillars feed on nontoxic plants in the custard apple family (Annonaceae). The adults are perfectly palatable but mimic distasteful butterflies. Different *Mimoides* species mimic other swallowtails or *Heliconius* longwings. The Peruvian Cattleheart Mimic (*Mimoides xynias*) mimics cattlehearts (*Parides* spp.), which are unpalatable swallowtails whose larvae store toxins from *Aristolochia*, their food plant. In some other *Mimoides* species the caterpillar is also a mimic, resembling a cattleheart larva so closely that the only easy way to distinguish it is by identifying the plant it is eating.

▲ *Lieinix nemesis*, Manu National Park, Peru
(Pieridae: Dismorphiinae)

Henry Walter Bates's observation that a number of South American
mimic whites (Dismorphiinae) looked extremely like some unpalatable tiger-patterned ithomiines led to the concept of Batesian mimicry (though some dismorphiines may be unpalatable themselves).
The Frosted Mimic White or Falcate Dismorphia (*Lieinix nemesis*),
though not a tiger mimic, could be mistaken for a clear-winged
ithomiine in flight, when the glossy sheen on the underside of its
drawn-out, hooked forewing glistens in the sunshine.

▲ *Perrhybris pamela*, male (l) and female (r), Manu
National Park, Peru (Pieridae: Pierinae)

Both sexes of Pamela (*Perrhybris pamela*) are unpalatable but only
one is a mimic. Except for its orange underwing stripe the male
looks like a typical white, but the female copies the tiger pattern
of *Mechanitis* and other ithomiines. In a number of butterflies –
primarily swallowtails and whites – the female is a mimic but the
male is not. Males may need a distinctive appearance to find a
mate, or the females may be more vulnerable as they search for
egg-laying sites and need the extra defense.

Surviving the Winter

Butterflies range as far as flowering plants grow, to the edges of glaciers and the heights of alpine tundra both north and south of the equator. For butterflies to occupy the temperate zone and to live there successfully, they have had to adapt to both cold temperatures and, critically, the passage of the seasons. No active butterfly can survive a temperate winter. In one form or another they either have to enter diapause, passing the winter in a state of suspended animation, or leave.

Migration has rigors of its own, and for many butterflies overwintering has been the better strategy. Out of 60 species of British butterflies, 9 overwinter as eggs, 33 as caterpillars, 11 as pupae and 8 as adults. One, the Speckled Wood (*Pararge aegeria*), can overwinter as either a larva or a pupa. Overwintering adults are usually the first butterflies to appear in spring, sometimes flying when snow and ice are still on the ground.

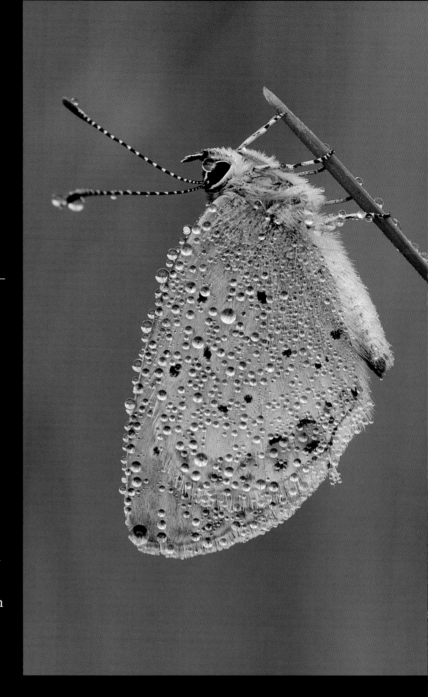

▲ *Cupido argiades*, Switzerland (Lycaenidae: Polyommatinae)
Active adult butterflies need a body temperature between 28° and 42°C (82°–108°F). In cool weather this Short-tailed Blue (*Cupido argiades*) may be able to do little more than wait. Though tropical butterflies may need to seek shade or adopt postures that reduce their exposure to direct sunlight, in cool weather temperate butterflies must bask in the sun or choose a warm spot to build up heat. By basking, a butterfly can raise its body temperature as much as 15°C (8.3°F) above that of the surrounding air.

▲ *Nymphalis antiopa*, Alps, Switzerland (Nymphalidae: Nymphalinae)

When autumn approaches, adult Mourning Cloaks (*Nymphalis antiopa*) seek shelter under a piece of bark or a shingle, or in a hollow tree, animal burrow, cave or unheated cellar. As the temperature drops, they fall into a stupor. Increased levels of sugars and glycerols in their cells act as a natural antifreeze as they pass the winter. In that condition Mourning Cloaks in Alaska did not freeze until temperatures reached −30°C (−22°F).

Monarchs in Winter

Many butterflies migrate, but it is the journeys of vast numbers of Monarchs (*Danaus plexippus*) that have captured the imagination of scientists and the public. Monarchs from west of the Rockies winter in southern California. The search for the wintering grounds of the far larger eastern population took famed Monarch biologist Fred Urquhart almost 40 years. In 1937 Dr. Urquhart found a way to attach a paper tag to the butterflies' wings without harming them or interfering with their journey. The tag read simply: "Send to Zoology University of Toronto Canada." For years he and a team that grew to thousands of volunteers tracked the butterflies' path, tagging the butterflies and pinpointing the location of each recovered tag.

▶ *Danaus plexippus*, Michoacan, Mexico (Nymphalidae: Danaiinae)
The tracks led to the mountains of Mexico. In January 1975, after a two-year search, Ken Brugger and his wife, Catalina Aguado, discovered the Monarchs' retreat. Butterflies by the millions, from 100 million hectares (247,000 acres) of breeding range, had converged on less than 8 hectares (20 acres) of mountain forest on Cerro Pelón, on the border between the states of México and Michoacan. Dr. Urquhart rushed to the site. To his astonishment, he found a butterfly bearing one of his tags; it had been applied by a volunteer far away in Minnesota.

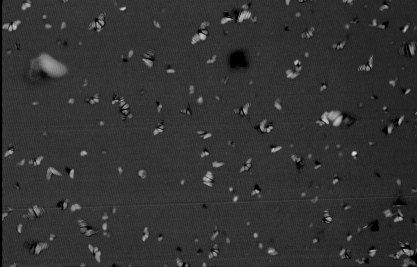

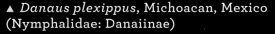

▲ *Danaus plexippus*, Michoacan, Mexico
(Nymphalidae: Danaiinae)
Other wintering sites were later discovered on nearby mountains.
Not all of these have survived. In 2002 it was estimated that 44% of
the best overwintering forest had been lost or degraded by illegal
logging. A number of wintering colonies vanished, while others
shrank alarmingly. Today Cerro Pelón is part of the 56,259-hectare
(139,000-acre) Monarch Butterfly Biosphere Reserve, established
in 2000 as a successor to earlier reserves. The reserve contains
most of the Monarchs' wintering colonies and was listed as a World
Heritage Site in 2008.

▲ *Danaus plexippus*, Michoacan, Mexico
(Nymphalidae: Danaiinae)
Strict law enforcement has paid off, coupled with financial support
that provides conservation incentives and alternative income sources,
including trout farming, for local communities. Six tourism cen-
ters now attract thousands of visitors every year. Large-scale illegal
logging has declined and was not detected at all in 2012. Small-scale
logging, though, continues. Monarchs still suffer from loss of breeding habitat, declines in milkweed populations and an increasingly
unstable climate. If they are to continue to assemble in the mountains
of Mexico, much needs to be done throughout their range.

At night, butterflies yield the skies to a host of moths. In numbers of species they outnumber butterflies by at least fifteen to one. Butterflies, which are themselves day-flying moths, are only one branch of a single advanced moth lineage. The vast array of other moths represents an enormous range of lifestyles. Many are serious agricultural pests, but others, including the Silk Moth (*Bombyx mori*), have provided humans with goods and income for thousands of years.

Most moths are tiny and, to the average eye, unremarkable. Some are among the most spectacular of all Lepidoptera, butterflies not excepted. There are blood-sucking moths, "primitive" moths with chewing mouthparts instead of coiled tongues, and adult moths with no mouthparts at all. There are wingless moths and moths whose wingspan exceeds that of any butterfly. There are moths that use ultrasonic sounds to find mates, and moths that use these sounds to escape bats by jamming their echolocation systems.

This chapter can give only a taste of the overwhelming majority of Lepidoptera. It is a miscellany, not a survey, from a vast world that to most of us is largely hidden in darkness.

▶ *Attacus atlas*, Malaysia (Saturniidae: Saturniinae)
Male giant silkmoths (Family Saturniidae), including one of the largest of them all, the Atlas Moth (*Attacus atlas*) of Southeast Asia, carry the most spectacular and complex antennae in the moth world. Their antennae can detect a single windborne molecule of female pheromone from up to 20 miles away. They need that sensitivity, for they have little time: adult silkmoths have no functional mouthparts, cannot feed, and live for only a few days.

Night-flying moths must court in the dark. The males still hunt for females, but instead of finding them by sight, as most butterflies do, they follow a chemical trail. Unlike butterflies, many female moths "call" to males by releasing far-carrying pheromones from glands in their abdomens. Males pick up the chemical calls from enormous distances, often on huge, multibranched, feathery antennae, and follow them in increasing concentrations to where the female awaits. A calling female moth may release a number of different chemicals, but usually only one acts as a long-distance lure. The others may function for short-range communication, particularly on contact, once the male arrives.

▲▲ Unidentified moth, Chocó, West Ecuador
▲ *Dirphia* sp, Central Ecuador (Saturniidae: Hemileucinae)
◣ Unidentified moth, Central Ecuador
▶ Unidentified moth, Kakamega Forest, Kenya
Even night-flying moths, like these from the cloud forests of Ecuador (top, above, and facing page top), and Kenya's Kakamega Forest (facing page right) can be colorful. Their bodies are often densely haired, insulating them against the night air. Moth antennae lack the terminal knobs that characterize those of butterflies. They are frequently feather-like, the better to pick up pheromones from calling females or plant compounds that may lead them to sources of food (for those that eat) or places to lay their eggs.

▲ *Saturnia pavonia*, Switzerland
(Saturniidae: Saturniinae)
▼ *Saturnia pyri*, Switzerland
(Saturniidae: Saturniinae)
◄ *Graellsia isabellae*, Switzerland
(Saturniidae: Saturniinae)
The males of these European silkmoths – the
Emperor Moth (*Saturnia pavonia*) (top), Great
Peacock Moth (*S. pyri*) (middle) and Spanish
Moon Moth (*Graellsia isabellae*) (bottom) – bear
antennae so sensitive to the lure of a female that
pheromone-baited traps are an excellent way to
monitor their presence. The sex pheromone of
the Spanish Moon Moth, a protected species con-
fined to the mountains of France and Spain, has
been used to detect and survey its populations as
part of its conservation.

▶ *Bathyphlebia emi-nens male*, Central Ecuador (Saturniidae: Ceratocampinae)

This is a male *Bathyphlebia eminens*, photographed in the cloud forest of central Ecuador. Its antennae, though impressive, are not as large as those on the males of some other large silkmoths. The antennae of female *Bathyphlebia* are even narrower than those of the male; since the males come to them, silkmoth females do not need to detect pheromones at a distance. Female silkmoths are also larger and heavier-bodied than the males – they need the extra size to store their eggs.

▶ *Rhodinia fugax shaanxiana*, Qinling Mountains, Shaanxi, China (Saturniidae: Saturniinae)

A male silkmoth needs not only to detect female pheromones, but to tell which ones come from its own species. The antennae of the male Squeaking Silkmoth (*Rhodinia fugax*) of China and Japan are sensitive to a specific chemical component released by a female of their own species, but do not react to the different, but related, compound that attracts males of another Japanese silkmoth, *Loepa sakaei*, to their females.

Moths Great and Small

Silkmoths

The giant silkmoths are creatures of wonder: large, spectacular and, as adults, ephemeral, with an almost ghostly beauty. The family to which they belong, the Saturniidae, includes more than 1,400 species worldwide (860 in Central and South America), divided into seven subfamilies. Though silkmoths take their name from their silken cocoons, commercial silk comes from *Bombyx mori*, a moth in a different family (Bombycidae).

◀ *Rothschildia hesperus*, Cacao, Roura, French Guiana (Saturniidae: Saturniinae)

Rothschildia hesperus is a South American relative of the Asian Atlas moths (*Attacus* spp.). Like them, *Rothschildia* moths have large clear areas in their wings, which is why they are known as *cuatro ventanas*, or "four windows," in Costa Rica. The scales on these windows are reduced to fine, hair-like bristles that reflect light when viewed from the side. Transparent when viewed on a perched moth, the windows can flash like mirrors as it flies in the moonlight. What they may be signaling is not fully understood.

▲ *Bathyphlebia eminens*, Central Ecuador (Saturniidae: Ceratocampinae)

Bathyphlebia is a South American genus related to the imperial moths (*Eacles* spp.). *Eacles* includes the Imperial Moth (*E. imperialis*), a widespread North American saturniid and one of several to have undergone dramatic declines in northeastern North America. It had disappeared from much of New England by the 1980s, possibly as a result of introduction of a parasitoid fly intended to combat infestations of Gypsy Moth (*Lymantria dispar*). It survives on Martha's Vineyard, Massachusetts, where the fly is apparently absent.

Moon Moths

Silkmoths have evolved long tails at least four different times. Some of these tails are truly extraordinary, as long as or longer than the moth itself. Why does a nocturnal moth need such ornaments? A recent study by Jesse Barber of Boise State University, Idaho, provides a surprising answer: the tails of the North American Luna Moth (*Actias luna*) distract bats. The echolocating signals bats use to find their prey bounce off the tails of flying moths, causing the bats to misdirect their strikes. Big Brown Bats (*Eptesicus fuscus*) caught only 35% of Luna Moths released in a darkened room, but the number rose to 81% if Barber cut off the moths' tails first. High-speed infrared videography showed that more than half of the bats attacked intact moths at the wrong end, and they missed almost every time.

▼ *Graellsia isabellae*, Switzerland
(Saturniidae: Saturniinae)
The Spanish Moon Moth (*Graellsia isabellae*) is a highly localized insect, confined to mountain pine forests in Spain, France and Switzerland. It is protected under the European Union Habitats Directive. Its caterpillars feed on pine needles, and once they have eaten a needle down to the stub, they seal the end with silk, presumably to protect themselves from the oozing resin.

▶ *Argema mittrei*
male, Madagascar
(Saturniidae:
Saturniinae)
The most spectacular of all
moon moths is probably the
male Comet Moth (*Argema
mittrei*) of Madagascar, with
its 20 cm (8 in) wingspan and
15 cm (6 in) tails (female tails
are broader and shorter). It is
uncommon in the wild but is
being raised locally in cap-
tivity to supply moth fanciers
and, with a number of other
Malagasy moths, as a potential
source of indigenously produced silk. Comet Moths lay
some of the largest eggs of any
known lepidopteran: up to 4
mm across.

Hawk moths, or sphinxes (Sphingidae), with their long, narrow forewings and large abdomens, are among the easiest to recognize of the larger moths. The family contains almost 1,500 species worldwide, divided among three subfamilies. Many fly by day, and a number mimic bees and wasps. Many hawk moths are active nectar-feeders, and many have long (sometimes very long), well-developed tongues. The record goes to a tropical American hawk moth, *Amphimoea walkeri*, whose proboscis measures 28 cm (11 in) – four times its body length.

Hawk moths are powerful fliers, and unlike most butterflies they can hover in front of a flower when feeding.

Their hovering ability may partly explain why their tongues can be so much longer than those of butterflies. A butterfly must normally alight to feed, and inserting a very long proboscis into a flower may be unmanageable from a perch. Hovering hawk moths can insert their tongues from a manageable distance and, perhaps, avoid spiders waiting for them among the flowers.

One European sphinx, the Death's-head Hawkmoth (*Acherontia atropos*), bears a marking on its thorax that resembles a human skull. It has long been feared as an omen of death. Its scientific name refers to the River Acheron in Hades and to Atropos, the Fate that cut the thread of life.

◄ *Protambulyx goeldii*, French Guiana (Sphingidae: Smerinthinae)
▲ *Batocnema cocquereli*, Madagascar (Sphingidae: Smerinthinae)
Protambulyx goeldii (left) is a member of a Central and South American genus with particularly long forewings that are characteristically notched at the tip. One *Protambulyx* species, the Streaked Sphinx (*P. strigilis*), ranges north to southern Florida. *Batocnema cocquereli* (above) is one of a number of hawk moths restricted to Madagascar. The only other *Batocnema* species, *B. africana*, is widespread in Africa. Both moths are members of the Smerinthinae, or eyed sphinx moths. They share scalloped, disruptively patterned wings that make them difficult to see against the bark of a tree.

▲ *Macroglossum stellata-*
rum, Switzerland (Sphingidae:
Macroglossinae)

▶ *Hemaris fuciformis*, Switzerland
(Sphingidae: Macroglossinae)

The Macroglossinae includes day-flying short-winged hawk moths that bear a remarkable resemblance to hovering hummingbirds as they seek nectar with outstretched tongues. They include the Hummingbird Hawkmoth (*Macroglossum stellatarum*) (left), here feeding at a Fuller's Teasel (*Dipsacus fullonum*). It is not a mimic, as it lives in Eurasia, where hummingbirds are absent. However, the Broad-bordered Bee Hawkmoth (*Hemaris fuciformis*) (right) and its kin, which have large clear areas in their wings, do mimic the appearance and flight of bumblebees.

▲ *Xanthopan morgani praedicta*, Madagascar
(Sphingidae: Sphinginae)

In 1862 Charles Darwin received a specimen of *Angraecum ses-quipidale*, an orchid from Madagascar with a nectar spur 20 to 30 cm (8–12 in) long. In a letter Darwin called it "astounding" and exclaimed, "Good Heavens what insect can suck it?" He later wrote: "in Madagascar there must be moths with proboscides capable of extension to a length of between ten and eleven inches!" In 1903, 20 years after Darwin's death, the description of *Xanthopan morgani praedicta*, now known as Darwin's Moth, proved him right.

◄ *Xanthopan morgani praedicta*, Madagascar
(Sphingidae: Sphinginae)

Darwin's great insight was that the orchid and the still-unknown moth must have evolved together, a process now called coevolution: "It would appear that there has been a race in gaining length between the nectary of the *Angraecum* and the proboscis of certain moths." The orchid gained an exclusive pollinator and the moth a source of nectar that only it could reach. It was not until 1992 – 130 years after his prediction – that scientists actually saw a Darwin's Moth feeding from its special orchid.

Day-flying Moths

A surprising number of moths are as active by day as butterflies. Many are every bit as colorful too, if not more so. A number of moth families are primarily day-flying, and some of the most colorful among them carry their colors as a warning that they are loaded with toxic chemicals.

◤ *Urania leilus*, Rurrenabaque, Bolivia (Uraniidae: Uraniinae)
▶ *Alcides zodiaca*, The Boulders, Australia (Uraniidae: Uraniinae)
The most spectacular day-flying moths belong to the tropical family Uraniidae. Insects such as the Swallowtail Moth (*Urania leilus*) of South America (top) and the Zodiac Moth (*Alcides zodiaca*) of tropical Australia (right) are easy to mistake for swallowtail butterflies. Indeed, some uraniids are involved, either as models or as mimics, in mimicry complexes with actual swallowtails. *Urania fulgens*, another tropical American species, is a migrant, flying several thousand kilometers every fall from Central into South America, with frequent stops for nectar en route.

◄ *Zygaena filipendulae*, Switzerland (Zygaenidae: Zygaeninae)

▲ Forester moth sp., Tangkoko Nature Reserve, North Sulawesi, Indonesia (Zygaenidae)

▶ *Zygaena filipendulae* (left) and *Zygaena lonicerae* (right), Switzerland (Zygaenidae: Zygaeninae)

◢ *Zygaena fausta*, Switzerland (Zygaenidae: Zygaeninae)

Burnets, or foresters (Family Zygaenidae), are highly toxic, containing glucosides that degrade into hydrogen cyanide. Their warning colors announce the fact. Unwary of predators, they are easily caught as they perch on flower heads. The sugar-packed crops of European burnets, including the Six-spot Burnet (*Zygaena filipendulae*) (left), the Auspicious Burnet (*Z. fausta*) (right) and the Narrow-bordered Five-spot Burnet (*Z. lonicerae*) (top right), can be easily removed from the moths. They contain little or no cyanide and were once a traditional childhood snack in northeastern Italy.

◄ *Tyria jacobaeae*, Reusstal,
Switzerland (Erebidae: Arctiinae)
◣ *Callimorpha dominula*, Switzerland
(Erebidae: Arctiinae)
▼ *Amata phegea*, Switzerland
(Erebidae: Arctiinae)

Tiger moths (Arctiinae) include a number of
toxic, warningly colored day-flying species,
as well as moths that mimic wasps. Even their
eggs can contain toxic chemicals, passed on
by their mothers. Caterpillars of the Cinnabar
Moth (*Tyria jacobaeae*) (top left) and the Scarlet
Tiger (*Callimorpha dominula*) (center), like
milkweed butterflies, take up pyrrolizidine
alkaloids, while the Nine-spotted Moth (*Amata
phegea*) (lower left) relies instead on defen-
sive proteins. All three moths are common
in Europe, and the Cinnabar Moth has been
introduced in New Zealand.

▲ *Dysphania sagana isolate* and *Dysphania trans-ducta*, Gunung Leuser National Park, Sumatra, Indonesia (Geometridae: Geometrinae)

The looper family, Geometridae, though related to both urani-ids and butterflies, is primarily nocturnal. The false tiger moths (*Dysphania* spp.) of eastern Asia to northeastern Australia are dis-tinctive and conspicuous exceptions. The Yellow Moth (*D. sagana*) is bred by Cambodian farmers, in part for a butterfly center in Siem Reap that has been operating since 2008. This photograph, taken in Sumatra, shows a silvery blue *D. transducta*, a species active both night and day, with several Yellow Moths.

◀ ▲ *Alytarchia leonina*, Gombe Stream
National Park, Tanzania (Erebidae: Arctiinae)
Alytarchia leonina is a widespread African tiger moth.
Moths do not normally roost en masse as some butterflies
do, but, like a number of other tiger moths, *A. leonina*
may gather in some numbers. This roost is in Tanzania's
Gombe Stream National Park, made famous by Jane
Goodall's chimpanzee research. If roosting tiger moths
are disturbed, they fly up in a cloud of wings. The effect
may be enough to startle a hungry predator if the toxins
the moths carry haven't already warned it off.

Giants

What is the largest moth, or, indeed, the largest lepidopteran? It depends on how you measure it. The largest insects, be they butterflies, moths or beetles (not to mention the largest spiders, millipedes and scorpions), all live in the tropics. We don't know why, but one idea is that warmer temperatures may be necessary for really big insects. The bigger they are, the more heat they may need to keep their metabolic rate high enough to survive. Though there were larger land invertebrates in the oxygen-rich atmosphere of the distant past, under the conditions in the world today these giant moths may be as big as insects can get.

▲ *Thysania agrippina*, Guyana (Noctuidae: Catocalinae)
◀ *Attacus atlas* male, Malaysia (Saturniidae: Saturniinae)
The tropical American White Witch (*Thysania agrippina*) (top), a member of the owlet moth family (Noctuidae), has the largest wingspan of any moth or butterfly: 31 cm (12.2 in). Female Atlas Moths (*Attacus atlas*) (bottom) of tropical Asia and Hercules Moths (*Coscinocera hercules*) of New Guinea and northeastern Australia have smaller spans – 26 and 27 cm (10.2 and 10.6 in) – but larger wing areas and heavier bodies. They usually share the title. Male Atlas Moths, like the males of other silkmoths, are smaller than the females.

The Tiny Majority

Though giant silkmoths and other large moths may catch our attention, the vast majority of moths are small. Some are minute: pygmy leaf miners (Family Nepticulidae) have a wingspan of as little as 2.5 mm. Their caterpillars are tiny enough to burrow within the thickness of a leaf, their passage betrayed only by the trails they leave. Moths in this size range are usually referred to as microlepidoptera, or micro-moths, though the distinction between the many micro-moth families and the larger moths, or macrolepidoptera, is largely for convenience. Among the micro-moths are the most ancient moth lineages, including four families of moths that have retained the chewing mandibles of other insects instead of evolving a coiled proboscis.

▲ *Coryptilum* sp., Crater Mountain, Papua New Guinea (Tineidae)
Most micro-moths are unobtrusive creatures patterned in mottled brown or gray, the better to camouflage themselves against twigs, rocks or dead leaves. This day-flying *Coryptilum* species from Papua New Guinea belongs to an unusually colorful genus in the clothes-moth family (Tineidae) that ranges from tropical Asia to Australasia. Tineid caterpillars, with only about a dozen exceptions, do not feed on living higher plants. Instead, the caterpillars of most of the 3,000 or so tineid species eat lichen, fungus, plant or animal debris or, of course, clothing.

▲ *Pterophorus pentadactyla*, Switzerland (Pterophoridae: Pterophorinae)
The White Plume Moth (*Pterophorus pentadactyla*) of Europe is one of the most distinctive of the Pterophoridae, a family of some 1,300 known species whose wings are usually split into fringed plumes. It is also one of the largest, with a wingspan of up to 3.5 cm (1.4 in). Its caterpillars feed on Bindweed (*Convulvulus arvensis*). Plume moths are mostly night-flying. When perched, many species hold their wings rolled and outstretched; they could pass for a bit of dried grass – or an extremely tiny airplane.

◀ *Oncocera semirubella*, Switzerland (Pyralidae: Phycitinae)
The snout moths (Pyralidae) include about 16,500 described species. Their caterpillars include leaf rollers and miners, root feeders and stem borers, and the family includes a large number of agricultural pests. The Rosy-striped Knot-horn (*Oncocera semirubella*) is one of the more attractive members of the family, with a wingspan ranging from 17 to 29 mm. It is active both by day and at night. In Britain it is confined to chalk downs and limestone cliffs in the south of England, where it is scarce.

The Wings of Moths

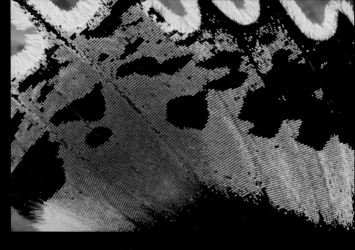

▲ *Chrysiridia rhipheus* hindwing detail, Madagascar
(Uraniidae: Uraniinae)

No moth or butterfly can match the display of structural colors on
the wings of the Madagascan Sunset Moth (*Chrysiridia rhipheus*),
created as light passes and reflects through and between its multi-
layered scales. Each scale alternates four or five sheets of cuticle,
separated by tiny rods, with intervening air spaces. Fine variations
in detail create the range of colors we see. Sunset Moths are bred
locally for sale, though for the Malagasy a moth emerging from its
silken cocoon evokes a spirit rising from a tomb.

◀ *Rhodinia fugax
shaanxiana* female,
Qinling Mountains,
Shaanxi province,
China (Saturniidae:
Saturniinae)

A female Squeaking Silkmoth
(*Rhodinia fugax shaanxiana*) on
a forest floor in China blends
perfectly with a bed of autumn
leaves. From a distance the
eyespots on her wings may
look like holes in a rotting leaf,
but at close range they may
startle predators, much as the
separately evolved eyespots
of nymphalid butterflies have
been shown to do. Some have
seen in her combination of eyespots and furry body the face
of a cat; but whether a predator
sees the same thing may be
impossible to tell.

► *Adhemarius dariensis*, Chiripo National Park, Costa Rica (Sphingidae: Smerinthinae)

In a number of moths, including underwing moths (Erebidae) and many hawk moths, the subtle camouflage patterns and colors on the body and forewings contrast startlingly with brilliant contrastingly colored and patterned hindwings. The function of this contrast is surely surprise. When perched normally, moths such as the Mexican and Central American *Adhemarius dariensis* conceal their bright colors beneath their folded hindwings. When disturbed, they flick their forewings open, exposing the hindwings to view.

▼◄ *Smerinthus ocellata*, Switzerland (Sphingidae: Smerinthinae)

The effect is even more startling when the hindwings reveal a pair of owl-like eyespots, as they do in the Eyed Hawkmoth (*Smerinthus ocellata*) of Europe. When disturbed, the previously passive moth raises its forewings, exposes its eyespots and bobs and trembles convulsively. Niko Tinbergen, a pioneer in the study of animal behavior, found that small songbirds, which are preconditioned to avoid hawks and owls, were frightened by this display into leaving the moth alone. However, they would attack it if the eyespots were obscured.

▲ *Automeris watsoni*, French Guiana
(Saturniidae: Hemileucinae)
◀ ◣ *Gamelia* sp. female, Tambopata
National Reserve, Peru (Saturniidae:
Hemileucinae)
The eyespots on the hindwings of the American
silkmoth genera *Automeris*, *Gamelia* and their
relatives are truly startling: large, conspicuous
and often surrounded by bright colors. At rest
the hindwings are hidden by the forewings, but
they are quickly exposed if the moth is disturbed.
The resemblance to a staring owl, enhanced by
lines suggesting the bird's facial disk, is remarkable (look at these photos upside down). Many
Automeris species accompany this revelation by
falling to the ground and performing a shivering,
wing-flicking dance.

Moth Life History

▼ *Saturnia pavonia*, Switzerland
(Saturniidae: Saturniinae)

A female Emperor Moth (*Saturnia pavonia*), the only silkmoth resident in Britain, emerges from her cocoon heavily laden with eggs. Once males, which fly by day, have arrived to fertilize her as she rests near her cocoon, she begins laying her clutches nearby – here, on Blackthorn (*Prunus spinosa*). As her load lightens, she flies by night to more distant locations, exhausting her supply of eggs in two or three days. She cannot feed, and will live only a few days longer.

Moth Caterpillars

Moth caterpillars, like moth adults, are tremendously varied in appearance and size. Many, including caterpillars that bore inside stems or roots, are plain-looking creatures. The caterpillars of micro-moths, of course, are tiny and easy to overlook. Some moth caterpillars, though, are large, striking insects, ranging from the highly colorful to the extremely bizarre. They have a remarkable array of defenses, and a few are even deadly to humans.

◄ ▲ *Saturnia pyri*, Switzerland
(Saturniidae: Saturniinae)

Mature caterpillars of the largest moth in Europe, the Giant Peacock Moth (*Saturnia pyri*), are decorated with sky-blue growths, or scoli, studded with hollow black bristles (left). If the caterpillar is disturbed, the bristles discharge a secretion containing glycerol and phenols which may repel attacking ants or birds. Threatened caterpillars use their mandibles to make a series of high-pitched chirps that may warn predators of their chemical defenses. Note the well-developed, contrastingly colored false legs, or prolegs, beneath the abdomen (above).

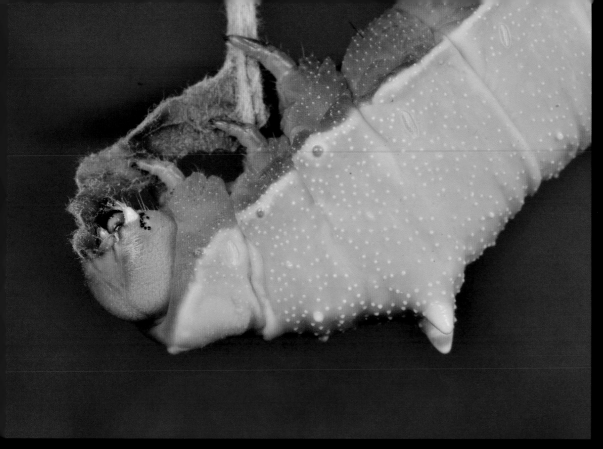

◀ *Rhodinia fugax shaanxiana*, Qinling Mountains, Shaanxi province, China (Saturniidae: Saturniinae)

Mature Squeaking Silkmoth (*Rhodinia fugax*) caterpillars are light green above and darker below. They usually crawl upside down, so their pattern acts as countershading. The spectral reflectance of their skin matches that of the oak leaves on which they feed. Green combines blue and yellow; however, exposure to light stimulates accumulation of blue but not yellow pigment. A caterpillar kept in the dark turns yellow but in bright sun stays green, matching, perhaps, the effect of light on the leaves. If their camouflage fails, disturbed caterpillars squeak like mice.

▶ *Acherontia atropos* (Sphingidae: Sphinginae)

Most hawk moth caterpillars, including the Death's-head Hawkmoth (*Acherontia atropos*) of Europe, can be recognized by their most prominent feature: a long "horn" arising from the end of the abdomen. Silkmoth and hawk moth caterpillars both eat leaves, sometimes from the same trees, but silkmoths often feed on older leaves while hawk moths prefer younger ones. Silkmoth mandibles are simple structures, good for cutting out bits of leaf, while the rough-toothed mandibles of hawk moths are better at tear- . ing, crushing and chewing.

▲ *Sphinx pinastri*,
Switzerland (Sphingidae:
Sphinginae)
◄ *Actias dubernardi*,
China (Saturniidae:
Saturniinae)
The first line of defense for
most moth caterpillars is
camouflage. Both the Pine
Hawkmoth (*Sphinx pinastri*) and
the Chinese Moon Moth (*Actias
dubernardi*), a silkmoth, have
caterpillars that feed on conifer
needles. On both, in their late
instars, patterns of white or
silver lines break up the green
of their bodies. They appear to
be no more than another cluster
of needles.

▶▼ *Acronicta alni*, Switzerland (Noctuidae: Acronictinae)

The caterpillar of the Alder Moth (*Acronicta alni*) starts life disguised – very effectively – as a bird dropping. In its final instar, however, it is completely different: black with bold yellow stripes. This is not because it has adopted a new chemical defense; all its instars are distasteful to birds, not just the final one. The final instar may take on warning colors because the caterpillar must find a spot to pupate; it cannot masquerade as a bird dropping if it has to keep moving.

▲ *Dysphania fenestrata*, Australia (Geometridae: Geometrinae)

The caterpillars of false tiger moths (*Dysphania* spp.), including the Australian Four-o'clock Moth (*Dysphania fenestrata*), are as colorful as the adults: bright green or greenish yellow, spotted and banded with black and blue. Their bright colors are presumably a warning

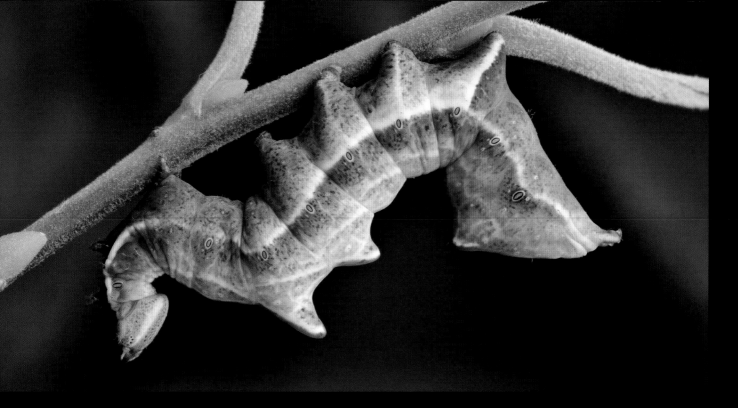

▲ *Notodonta ziczac*, Switzerland (Notodontidae: Notododontinae)

When the caterpillar of a Pebble Prominent (*Notodonta ziczac*), a common European member of the prominent family (Notodontidae), is threatened, it raises its head and the end of its abdomen. You might be forgiven for wondering which end is which. The tail end (on the right) is far larger and more brightly colored. Its peculiar shape may make the insect hard to recognize as a caterpillar, particularly in its threat posture.

▶ *Stauropus fagi*, Switzerland (Notodontidae: Heterocampinae)

The late-instar larva of the Lobster Moth (*Stauropus fagi*), even more than the Pebble Prominent, is almost unrecognizable as a caterpillar. When disturbed its head and tail touch, resulting in a shape like a disintegrating dead leaf. If detected, it thrusts its extremely long legs out and forward, but whether this startles birds is unknown. First-instar larvae are black; they copy the appearance and behavior of ants, wiggling their long legs in a very ant-like manner. They acquire their leaf-like appearance as they grow and molt.

▶ *Cerura vinula*, Switzerland (Notodontidae: Notododontinae)

If a Puss Moth (*Cerura vinula*) caterpillar is threatened, it raises and retracts its head to reveal a pinkish "face," lifts its "tails" (highly modified anal, or rear, prolegs) and lashes them about while extruding a whip-like pinkish filament from each. If that doesn't work, it can squirt a formic acid solution from a gland beneath its head – very painful if it gets in your eye. All this display is directed less at birds, which eat the caterpillars anyway, than at parasitic wasps and flies.

Caterpillars from at least 10 moth families are armed with stinging, or urticating, hairs (as in *Urtica*, the stinging nettle). Their effect can range from irritating and painful to extremely dangerous, leading to anaphylactic shock, hemorrhaging, and even death. Stinging caterpillars are usually brightly colored and conspicuous, a warning to any parasite or predator that approaches them.

▲ Flannel moth caterpillar, Tingo Maria, Peru (Megalopygidae)

Disturb a flannel moth caterpillar (Family Megalopygidae) and it may erupt into a bristling pompom of furry hairs. Its threat is not to be taken lightly. Concealed in the dense erect fur are toxic needle-like bristles that can break off in your skin, releasing toxins that cause excruciating pain. Most megalopygids live in the American tropics, where some species are up to 8 cm (3 in) long. Several reach the United States, where they outrank even the Saddleback Caterpillar in toxicity. The downy nestlings of a South American bird, the Cinereous Mourner (*Laniocera hypopyrra*), look and move like flannel moth caterpillars, and may be mimicking them as a way to deter predators.

◄ Slug caterpillar, Haia Village, Papua New Guinea (Limacodidae)

Slug caterpillars (Limacodidae) are among the most unusual of moth larvae. Their appearance is varied and bizarre. Many are highly colorful and armed with clusters of stinging hairs. Their prolegs are concealed and tipped with suckers, and instead of crawling they glide on their bellies. Their heads, covered by an extension of the thorax, are all but invisible. The sting of the Saddleback Caterpillar (*Acharia stimulea*), one of the most venomous in North America, can cause

◄ Automeris sp., Manu National Park, Peru (Saturniidae: Hemileucinae)
▼ ▶ *Automeris* sp., Manu National Park, Peru (Saturniidae: Hemileucinae)
◢ *Automeris* sp., Manu National Park, Peru (Saturniidae: Hemileucinae)

Automeris is a silkmoth genus known for its caterpillars' fearsome stings. Though most are tropical American, the larva of one, the Io Moth (*A. io*), is the best-known stinging caterpillar in North America. Io Moth caterpillars are covered with bristles, each – like the urticating hairs of other stinging caterpillars – connected to a venom gland. The hairs break off easily on contact, and breaking the tip of a bristle releases its poison. These photographs display a few of the 200-odd *Automeris* species known from tropical America.

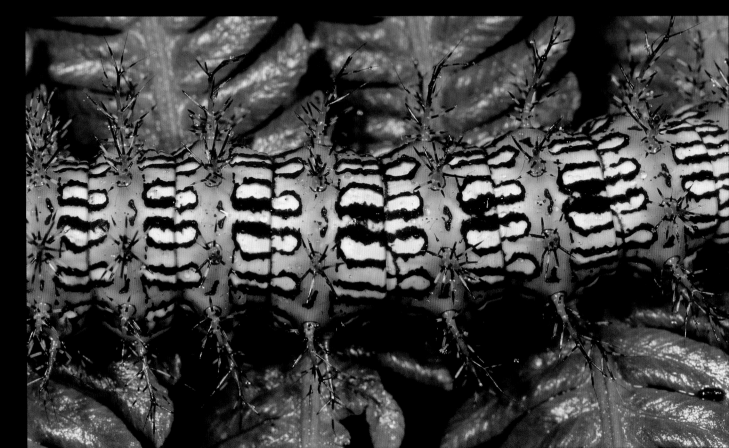

▲ *Rhodinia fugax shaanxiana* (Saturniidae: Saturniinae)

Unlike most butterflies, the majority of moths pupate within a silken cocoon, usually attached to a plant or in a burrow underground (most hawk moths pupate in shallow soil, often without spinning a cocoon). The structure and composition of cocoons vary greatly. One of the most attractive is the open-topped green cocoon of the Squeaking Silkmoth (*Rhodinia fugax*), which resembles the trap of a pitcher plant. The pupa nestles inside and a drainage hole at the bottom prevents the cocoon from filling with rainwater.

◀ *Sesia apiformis exuvium*, Switzerland (Sesiidae: Sesiinae)

The larva of the Hornet Moth (*Sesia apiformis*) bores into the wood of poplar trees. After one or two years it spins a cocoon of silk and debris in a chamber beneath the bark. It spends a further winter inside it and then pupates within the cocoon in early spring. To escape, the pupa wriggles out, using short bristles on its abdomen for purchase, until almost half of its body protrudes from the tree. Only then does it emerge as an adult, leaving its empty shell, or exuvium, behind.

▲ ▶ *Borocera* sp., Montagne des
Français Reserve, Antsiranana,
Madagascar (Lasiocampidae:
Gonometinae)

In Madagascar, *landibe*, or wild silk, has long
been made from the cocoons of native moths.
Silk from *Borocera cajani* was traditionally used to
make ritual burial shrouds. Harvesting, spinning, dyeing and weaving *Borocera* silk, which is
preferred in Madagascar over commercial silk for
both shrouds and clothing, provide a source of
income for local communities, especially before
the rice harvest. The pupae themselves are eaten
as a delicacy. Deforestation and overharvesting,
unfortunately, have greatly reduced both the
supply of wild cocoons and the income their silk
provides.

Camouflage, Masquerade and Mimicry

▲ **Unidentified moth, Chocó, West Ecuador**
◄ **Noctuid sp., French Guiana (Noctuidae)**
Moths are past masters at camouflage and masquerade. They can blend imperceptibly with the bark of a tree (left) or, by rolling their wings (above), pass themselves off as a dried stem, a scrap of bark or a twiglet. These are from South America.

▲ *Gastropacha quercifolia*, Switzerland
(Lasiocampidae: Pinarinae)

The Lappet (*Gastropacha quercifolia*) is one of the
most perfectly camouflaged of European moths.
Both its shape and its posture, with splayed
hindwings emerging from beneath the forewings,

▲ Unidentified moth, Chocó, West Ecuador

Besides being masters of camouflage, moths can be highly convincing mimics of
ants, beetles, spiders and other invertebrates that a predator might see as either
toxic or unpalatable. This moth from Ecuador has copied the basic shape and color
pattern of a firefly (Lampyridae); fireflies are known to carry noxious chemicals. Both
moth and firefly may be part of a larger mimicry complex that could include lookalike
soldier beetles, cockroaches and other insects.

▲ *Hemaris tityus*, Switzerland (Sphingidae: Macroglossinae)
◀ *Sesia apiformis*, Switzerland (Sesiidae: Sesiinae)
A number of day-flying moths are close mimics of bees and wasps. Both the Narrow-bordered Bee Hawkmoth (*Hemaris tityus*) (above), which resembles a bumblebee, and the Hornet Moth (*Sesia apiformis*) (left), an extremely effective mimic of large vespid wasps, adopt the lazy, buzzing flight of their models. The Hornet Moth is known to be distasteful to birds, so its appearance is both a masquerade and a warning. This one has extruded a pheromone-releasing gland from the tip of its abdomen.

▲ ▲ Unidentified looper, Tingo Maria, Peru
(Geometridae)
▲ possible *Xanthiris* sp., Peru (Geometridae:
Sterrhinae)
↘ *Atyriodes figulatum*, Manu National Park, Peru
(Geometridae: Sterrhinae)
↘ ↘ *Cyllopoda claudicula?*, Manu National Park, Peru
(Geometridae: Sterrhinae)

Day-flying moths are frequently involved in mimicry complexes
with butterflies. These four geometrid moths from Peru are part of
an extensive array of similar-looking black-and-yellow moths and
butterflies from at least seven different families, including skippers,
nymphalids and metalmarks as well as prominents, tiger moths
and others. They are often found flying or puddling together and
presumably benefit from their mutual resemblance, but which ones
(if any) are toxic or unpalatable and could be models for the others
(or one another) remains unknown.

A Miscellany of Moths

We close with two galleries of moths from the rainforests of South America. Some are mimics, some are masqueraders and some are undoubtedly flaunting colors that warn of toxic chemicals within their bodies. Undoubtedly a great many more remain to be discovered, providing we can get to them before their rainforest homes disappear.

1. *Rhipha flammans*, Cacao, Roura, French Guiana (Erebidae: Arctiinae)
2. *Gorgonidia buckleyi*, Cacao, Roura, French Guiana (Erebidae: Arctiinae)
3. *Polygrammodes* sp., Farallones de Cali, Colombia (Crambidae)
4. *Semaeopus nisa*, Farallones de Cali, Colombia (Geometridae: Sterrhinae)
5. Unidentified moth, Manu National Park, Peru
6. Looper sp., Manu National Park, Peru (Geometridae)

Unidentified moths, Chocó, West Ecuador

These moths all come from one place: the Chocó bioregion of northwestern Ecuador, one of the richest biodiversity hotspots on the planet and one of the most endangered. Ninety percent of the forest in the Ecuadorian portion of the Chocó has been cleared for agriculture. Today the UCLA-based Center for Tropical Research is combining education, research and work with local communities to save what is left. These brilliant little moths, not to mention the Chocó's birds and other wildlife, provide reason enough to do so.

Boggs, C.L., W.B. Watt and P.R. Ehrlich. *Butterflies: Ecology and Evolution Taking Flight*. Chicago: University of Chicago Press, 2003.

Braby, M.F. *The Butterflies of Australia: Their Identification, Biology and Distribution*. Collingwood, Australia: CSIRO, 2000.

———. *The Complete Field Guide to Butterflies of Australia*. Collingwood, Australia: CSIRO, 2004.

Brock, J.P., K. Kaufman and J.P. Brock. *Kaufman Field Guide to Butterflies of North America*. New York: Houghton Mifflin, 2003.

Cassie, B., and K.B. Sandved. *A World of Butterflies*. New York: Bulfinch, 2004.

Cech, R., and G. Tudor. *Butterflies of the East Coast: An Observer's Guide*. Princeton, NJ: Princeton University Press, 2005.

Collins, N.M., and M.G. Morris. *Threatened Swallowtail Butterflies of the World: The IUCN Red Data Book*. Gland, Switzerland: IUCN, 1985.

Covell, C.V. *A Field Guide to Moths of Eastern North America*. Martinsville: Virginia Museum of Natural History in association with the Smithsonian Institution, 2005.

d'Abrera, B. *World Butterflies*. London: Hill House, 2006.

DeVries, P.J. *The Butterflies of Costa Rica and Their Natural History*. 2 vols. Princeton, NJ: Princeton University Press, 1987 and 1997.

Ek-Amnuay, P. *Butterflies of Thailand*. Bangkok: Baan Lae Suan Amarin, 2012.

Glassberg, J. *Butterflies of North America*. New York: Sterling, 2011.

———. *A Swift Guide to the Butterflies of Mexico and Central America*. Morristown, NJ: Sunstreak, 2007.

———. *A Swift Guide to the Butterflies of North America*. Morristown, NJ: Sunstreak, 2012.

Guppy, C.S., J. Shepard and Royal British Columbia Museum. *Butterflies of British Columbia: Including Western Alberta, Southern Yukon, the Alaska Panhandle, Washington, Northern Oregon, Northern Idaho, Northwestern Montana*. Vancouver: UBC Press, 2001.

Halpern, S. *Four Wings and a Prayer: Caught in the Mystery of the Monarch Butterflies*. New York: Pantheon Books, 2001.

Hoskins, A. *Butterflies of the World*. London: New Holland, 2015.

Howse, P. *Butterflies: Messages from Psyche*. Winterbourne, UK: Papadakis, 2010.

Howse, P., and K. Wolfe. *The Giant Silkmoths: Colour, Mimicry and Camouflage*. Winterbourne, UK: Papadakis, 2012.

Khew, S.K. *A Field Guide to the Butterflies of Singapore*. Singapore: Ink on Paper, 2010.

Kirton, L. *A Naturalist's Guide to the Butterflies of Peninsular Malaysia, Singapore and Thailand*. Oxford: John Beaufoy, 2014.

Larsen, T.B. *The Butterflies of Kenya and Their Natural History*. Oxford: Oxford University Press, 1999.

Laufer, P. *The Dangerous World of Butterflies: The Startling Subculture of Criminals, Collectors, and Conservationists*. Guilford, CT: Lyons, 2009.

Layberry, R.A., P.W. Hall, J.D. Lafontaine and Canada Institute for Scientific and Technical Information. *The Butterflies of Canada*. Toronto: University of Toronto Press, 1998.

Marent, T., and B. Morgan. *Butterfly*. New York: DK Publishing, 2008.

Mikula, R., and C. Mikula. *Garden Butterflies of North America: A Gallery of Garden Butterflies and How to Attract Them*. Minocqua, WI: Willow Creek, 1997.

Miller, J.C., D.H. Janzen and W. Hallwachs. *100 Caterpillars: Portraits from the Tropical Forests of Costa Rica*. Cambridge, MA: Belknap, 2006.

Nash, D., T. Boyd and D. Hardiman. *Ireland's Butterflies: A Review*. Dublin: Dublin Naturalists' Field Club, 2012.

New, T.R. *Lepidoptera and Conservation*. Chichester, UK: Wiley, 2014.

Oberhauser, K.S., and M.J. Solensky. *Monarch Butterfly Biology and Conservation*. Ithaca, NY: Cornell University Press, 2004.

Opler, P.A. *A Field Guide to Eastern Butterflies*. Boston: Houghton Mifflin, 1998.

Opler, P.A., and J.W. Tilden. *A Field Guide to Western Butterflies*. Boston: Houghton Mifflin, 1999.

Orr, A.G., and R.L. Kitching. *The Butterflies of Australia*. Crows Nest, NSW: Allen & Unwin, 2011.

Preston-Mafham, K. *500 Butterflies: Butterflies from Around the World*. Rochester, UK: Grange, 2007.

Preston-Mafham, R., and K. Preston-Mafham. *Butterflies of the World*. London: Cassell, 2004.

Sbordoni, V., and S. Forestiero. *Butterflies of the World*. Buffalo, NY: Firefly, 1998.

Schappert, P.J. *A World for Butterflies: Their Lives, Behavior, and Future*. Buffalo, NY: Firefly, 2005.

Scott, J.A. *The Butterflies of North America: A Natural History and Field Guide*. Stanford, CA: Stanford University Press, 1992.

Speart, J. *Winged Obsession: The Pursuit of the World's Most Notorious Butterfly Smuggler*. New York: William Morrow, 2011.

Sterling, P., M. Parsons and R. Lewington. *Field Guide to the Micro Moths of Great Britain and Ireland*. Gillingham, UK: British Wildlife, 2012.

Tolman, T., and R. Lewington. *Butterflies of Europe*. Princeton, NJ: Princeton University Press, 2001.

Tyler, H.A., K.S. Brown and K.H. Wilson. *Swallowtail Butterflies of the Americas: A Study in Biological Dynamics, Ecological Diversity, Biosystematics, and Conservation*. Gainesville, FL: Scientific, 1994.

Wagner, D.L. *Caterpillars of Eastern North America: A Guide to Identification and Natural History*. Princeton, NJ: Princeton University Press, 2005.

———. *Owlet Caterpillars of Eastern North America*. Princeton, NJ: Princeton University Press, 2011.

Waring, P., M. Townsend, M. Tunmore and R. Lewington. *Field Guide to the Moths of Great Britain and Ireland*. Gillingham, UK: British Wildlife, 2009.

Woodhall, S. *Field Guide to Butterflies of South Africa*. Cape Town: Struik, 2005.

Young, M. *The Natural History of Moths*. London: Poyser, 1997.

SELECTED WEBSITES

Butterflies and Moths of North America: http://www.butterfliesandmoths.org/

Butterflies of America: http://butterfliesofamerica.com/

Butterflies of Singapore: http://butterflycircle.blogspot.ca/

Learn about Butterflies: http://www.learnaboutbutterflies.com/

Lepidoptera and Their Ecology [Europe]: http://www.pyrgus.de/index_en.php

Monarch Watch: http://www.monarchwatch.org/

Nymphalidae Systematics Group: http://nymphalidae.utu.fi/Nymphalidae.htm

Samui Butterflies [Thailand]: http://www.samuibutterflies.com/home/

United Kingdom Butterfly Monitoring Scheme (UKBMS): http://www.ukbms.org/

The Xerces Society for Invertebrate Conservation: http://www.xerces.org/

Anyone interested in learning more is welcome to download a list of the 400+ papers consulted while writing this book. The link can be found at http://ronorensteinwriter.blogspot.ca/2015/04/referencelistforbutterflies.html.

Author's Acknowledgments

I am not an entomologist, and I am grateful for the help I received from those who are. Harald Krenn and Keith Willmott read over large sections of the text. Charles Covell read the chapter on moths, Steven Reppert the section on migration and Keith Wolfe the text on caterpillars. Shorter sections were reviewed by Tetsu Ando, Zsolt Bálint, Janne Valkonen and Roger Vila. I learned much from their comments and corrections.

Keith Willmott checked and corrected identifications for a number of tropical American butterflies, particularly for the difficult Tribe Ithomiini. Les Day did the same for butterflies from Southeast Asia. Keith Wolfe helped identify a number of caterpillar photographs, and Charles Covell, James Hayden and Bill Oehlke identified many of the moths. Rob de Vos, Efrain Hanao, Andrew Warren and Piet Zumkehr provided additional identifications.

Sylvia Fallon of the Natural Resources Defense Council brought me up to date on the NRDC lawsuit on behalf of Monarch Butterflies. I also benefited greatly from some highly informative butterfly sites on the Internet, including Les Day's Samui Butterflies and Adrian Hoskins' Learn About Butterflies. I have included their links in the reading list. Nonetheless, despite the valuable help I received from many people, the responsibility for any errors here is my own.

In general the classification used here follows that in the Tree of Life Project (http://tolweb.org/tree/). There is no globally accepted standard list of butterflies, and I have drawn English names from a variety of sources. When I could find none, I have used Latin names rather than coining yet another name in English.

Thanks to Thomas Marent for his many superb photographs. I am also grateful to Luc Legal for contributing the photographs of Short-horned Baronia (*Baronia brevicornis*), and to the Museum of Comparative Zoology, Harvard, and Conni O'Connor for the image of *Prodryas persephone*. My thanks to Lionel Koffler, Elizabeth McCurdy and Michael Mouland at Firefly Books, and to Linda Gustafson of Counterpunch Inc., for their help in putting this book together and for setting my words in such a beautiful package.

This book was written at a very difficult time for me and for my family. Shortly after the project began, my wife and I learned that our grandson Royce Raja Wong had been diagnosed with cancer. We spent much of the next five months by his bedside in Singapore, and we have since brought the family to Canada where Royce continues to receive treatment at the Hospital for Sick Children in Toronto. Less ideal conditions for writing a book of natural history it is hard to imagine. I am more than grateful to my wife Eileen Yen, and to the rest of our family, for making room for me to write and for tolerating my too-frequent absences at the computer. Thanks to my mother Mary Orenstein (who always loved butterflies), and to my children and grandchildren. A special thanks to our cousins Chris, Susan and Cynthia Chang who provided us with a home in Singapore, and were always ready to take me out to local nature reserves to refresh my mind and to rejoice in the presence of many of the butterflies you can find in these pages. This book is dedicated to Royce, in the hope that one day, when he is older and stronger, he will turn its pages with delight.

Photographer's Acknowledgments

I would like to thank my parents Rose and Richard Marent for their unending support and for understanding my time consuming passion of photographing and breeding butterflies and moths since my childhood.

I would also like to thank my friends David Weiller and Lukas Schwab for accompanying me on many trips in Switzerland and around the world.

Without them this book would not have been possible.

Finally I wish to thank Ron Orenstein and Michael Mouland for their great work on the book.